You decide that you can't afford to wait for Wolverine to return. If you are going to risk absorbing the mind of your ninja prisoner to discover his secrets, you might as well get it over with. You take a firm grip of your prisoner with one hand, yank off the glove on the other hand with your teeth, and touch your bare hand to his.

Caught completely unaware, the ninja's mind flows effortlessly into your own, but the thoughts there are so repulsive you almost wish he could have resisted you.

Your mind fills with visions of countless bodies that you—no, that *he*—has killed mercilessly. His mind does not even seem to be his own. He thinks only of a master who owns his soul. You grow sickened by his lust for death.

With horror, you realize that the Hand assassin's body, without its consciousness, is beginning to dissolve! *S'pose he's trapped inside me forever?* you think desperately as darkness envelops you.

Will the ninja's evil mind be trapped inside Rogue?

Make a Power Absorption FEAT by rolling one die and adding the result to your Power Absorption ability. If the total is 12 or less, turn to **86**. If it is 13 or more, turn to **143**.

Whatever the outcome, only your decisions,
and the luck of the die roll, can help save you from
AN X-CELLENT DEATH

Adventure Gamebook #7

AN X-CELLENT DEATH

BY KATE NOVAK

Illustrated by
John Statema and Mark A. Nelson

PUFFIN BOOKS
in association with TSR, Inc.

To my mother and father,
who always encouraged my mutant abilities

PUFFIN BOOKS

Published by the Penguin Group
27 Wrights Lane, London W8 5TZ, England
Viking Penguin Inc., 40 West 23rd Street, New York, New York 10010, USA
Penguin Books Australia Ltd, Ringwood, Victoria, Australia
Penguin Books Canada Ltd, 2801 John Street, Markham, Ontario, Canada L3R 1B4
Penguin Books (NZ) Ltd, 182–190 Wairau Road, Auckland 10, New Zealand

Penguin Books Ltd, Registered Offices: Harmondsworth, Middlesex, England

Created and first published in the USA by TSR, Inc.,
Lake Geneva, Wisconsin 1987
Published in Puffin Books 1989
1 3 5 7 9 10 8 6 4 2

Copyright © Marvel Entertainment Group, Inc., 1987
The Uncanny X-Men™ in *An X-cellent Death* by Kate Novak
copyright © Marvel Entertainments Group, Inc., 1987
All rights reserved

The names of characters used herein are fictitious and do not refer
to any persons living or dead. Any descriptions, including similarities
to persons living or dead, are merely coincidental.
All Marvel characters, character names, and the distinctive likenesses thereof,
are trademarks of the Marvel Entertainment Group, Inc.

Printed and bound in Great Britain by
Cox & Wyman Ltd, Reading

Except in the United States of America,
this book is sold subject to the condition
that it shall not, by way of trade or otherwise,
be lent, re-sold, hired out, or otherwise circulated
without the publisher's prior consent in any form of
binding or cover other than that in which it is
published and without a similar condition
including this condition being imposed
on the subsequent purchaser

FACE FRONT, TRUE BELIEVERS!

In this new role-playing gamebook, you are not one but FOUR of the Uncanny X-Men as, collectively, you face one of your most formidable foes in the Marvel Universe.

Based on the popular MARVEL SUPER HEROES® Role-Playing Game from TSR, Inc., MARVEL SUPER HEROES Adventure Gamebooks require only a single standard, six-sided die; a pen or pencil; a moderate supply of luck; and, most of all, your own personal skill in making decisions as you play the game. If dice are not available, you can consult page 12 for a simple alternative requiring only pencil and paper.

MARVEL SUPER HEROES Adventure Gamebooks have been designed to read easily, without complicated rules to slow down the story. Once you finish reading the rules that follow, you should seldom find it necessary to refer back to them. Your choices are clearly stated at each choice point, with occasional reminders of additional options you have available.

Your adventure reads like a book, plays like a game, and offers a thrill a minute—with YOU as your favorite MARVEL SUPER HEROES!

YOUR CHARACTERS

In this book, you play the parts of four members of the X-Men, a group of super-powered mutants forged into a team by Professor Charles Xavier for a dual purpose. Professor Xavier's intent was to form a group that, first, offered each individual member an opportunity to learn to control and use his or her powers safely, and, second, directed their team efforts against threats to mankind, whether from extraterrestrial aliens, other super-powered mutants, or power-hungry, evil human beings. Unfortunately, the team's efforts are not often recognized or even appreciated. The X-Men are considered to be outlaw vigilantes by many.

You will alternate between role-playing four important members of the X-Men team: Wolverine, Rogue, Nightcrawler, and Storm.

WOLVERINE has special characteristics that make him a truly formidable fighter. His bones are laced with a substance called adamantium, which makes them virtually unbreakable. In addition, he was surgically implanted with a set of six-inch claws of the same metal, which can slash through flesh with ease and harder substances with little difficulty. The Canadian-born Wolverine is known to possess a short temper.

ROGUE is one of the youngest members of the X-Men team, and her control over her powers is by no means complete. With her strange mutant ability of power absorption, she unintentionally stole all of the first Ms. Marvel's powers and memories. Thus Rogue is able to fly, has amazing strength, and possesses a nearly invulnerable body.

NIGHTCRAWLER is a natural teleporter. He was once a circus acrobat and is very agile. With a body covered with indigo fur, plus a long prehensile tail, he is the least human-looking member of the group. Nevertheless, he has a strong sense of ethics and considerable compassion, making him one of the most humane of all the X-Men.

STORM was once a potent weather witch, able to command the weather itself, but this ability was stolen from her when she got in the way of a mutant-power-draining weapon wielded by a bigoted government agent who was trying to subdue Rogue. Storm has remained as the leader of the X-Men despite the loss of her mutant powers, having proven her skill in leadership and her cunning in combat.

PLAYING THE GAME

The Marvel Super Heroes portrayed in this series of books have certain powerful abilities far beyond those of the average human being. Each character's special abilities, which will allow you to attempt feats a normal person wouldn't even consider, are listed on the removable **MARVEL SUPER HEROES Stats Card** located at the front of this book. The Stats Card lists everything you need to keep track of in order to play the game in this book. At the same time, it doubles as a handy bookmark.

SCORING

Playing the game requires that you keep track of three things—**Health points, Karma points**, and **Ability points**—on the MARVEL SUPER HERO Stats Card located at the front of this book. An explanation of each of these follows.

HEALTH POINTS

Health points represent your general health, or life strength. If you are injured or become ill, you lose some of these points. If you lose too many of these points, it will be harder for you to do some things. If you lose all of your Health points, you will fall unconscious and possibly even die. If any one of your four characters' Health points drop to 0, your adventure is over and you must begin again.

If you are hurt or sick, a teammate may administer first aid to you or you can rest. These will help you regain your Health points. Always remember, however, that it is not possible to regain more Health points than you had at the start of the game.

If at any time you are injured and must lose Health points, you may choose instead to substitute Karma points. This indicates a last superhuman effort you make to avoid damage. Simply subtract 1 Karma point for each Health point of loss. You may also choose to split the damage between Karma points and Health points. For example, if the instructions tell you to subtract 5 Health points, you may instead subtract 3 Health points and 2 Karma points. You must determine how to distribute damage immediately, however. You cannot change your mind about how to divide it after you continue reading. If you have already spent all your Karma points, you *must* subtract the damage from your Health points.

At the start of your adventure, Wolverine has 22 Health points, Rogue has 18, Nightcrawler 21, and Storm 21.

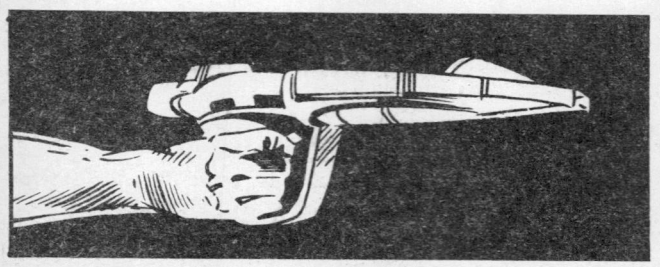

KARMA POINTS

Karma points represent the effects your actions will have on your future. You earn Karma by doing heroic deeds, by making the right decisions, and in general by being a good person. Conversely, if you do things you should not do, you may lose Karma.

You may spend Karma on any die roll you make to increase your chance of success. Here's how it works:

You must make your decision to spend Karma *before* you roll the die.

Once you commit yourself to spending Karma on a die roll, you *must* spend at least 1 Karma point. You may add as many more Karma points as you need to make your die roll successful, providing you have enough Karma points to spend.

If you decide to spend Karma on your die roll but fail the roll because you don't have enough Karma points to spend or because you choose not to spend that much Karma, you still lose the original 1 Karma point.

You can also spend Karma to keep yourself from being damaged, as explained under **HEALTH POINTS**.

There is no limit to the number of Karma points you can earn, but you will do better to spend your Karma rather than to hoard it. You can never have fewer than 0 Karma points. The X-Men's Karma points are held in a common pool; that is, all the Karma they earn is held in common and may be used by any individual of the team.

Your X-Men team—Wolverine, Rogue, Nightcrawler, and Storm—begins the adventure with 30 Karma points in their Karma Pool.

ABILITY POINTS

Ability points determine how easy or difficult it is for you to perform certain actions, called **FEATS**. Whenever you are asked to attempt a particular type of FEAT, consult the ability called for on your MARVEL SUPER HEROES Stats Card, roll one die, and add the result of the die roll to your Ability score. The text will indicate what you should do next, according to what your total was.

The abilities used in this gamebook are described below.

FIGHTING determines how good you are in armed and unarmed combat. When you are playing Wolverine, your Fighting ability is outstanding, while as Nightcrawler and Storm, you are only above average. In this game, Rogue has no listing for Fighting ability because she will rely on her other abilities. When you are Wolverine, you will sometimes fight with your adamantium claws and sometimes without them. As Wolverine, you must constantly remember that, although your claws make fighting easier, using them during combat could be fatal for your opponent, and unjustified killing could cost you Karma.

Agility is a measure of your coordination. This is an ability in which Nightcrawler excels. Agility is also one of your strengths when you play Rogue or Storm. No Agility points are listed for Wolverine, since it will be to his advantage to use his other skills. Agility determines how easily you can dodge out of the way of danger or catch something coming toward you.

Strength determines how much damage you inflict when you hit something. It also tells you how much weight you can lift. When you play Rogue, who has acquired the first Ms. Marvel's abilities, you have amazing Strength. No Strength points are listed for your teammates, however. Since their strengths are more or less human, they will rely on you when Strength is needed. As Rogue, you are aware that you must often pull your punches, because you are so strong that if you hit someone too hard, you could injure him or even kill him.

Intuition gauges how observant you are and how quickly you can react. When you are playing Wolverine, you have an Intuition beyond human ken. You are able to track an individual's scent, read body language, and even sense when something "feels" wrong. No Intuition is listed for the other X-Men, so they will be counting heavily on Wolverine.

Fast Healing is a specialized mutant ability of Wolverine's. His body is able to heal wounds with miraculous speed, and it is nearly immune to poisons and drugs. When you play Wolverine, this will help you keep from losing too many hit points.

Power Absorption is a specialized mutant ability of Rogue's. When you play Rogue, you have the ability to gain the powers, skills, and knowledge of an intelligent being you touch with your flesh. Unfortunately, you cannot control this ability. The absorption will take place whether you wish it to or not, so normally you keep your

gloves on. When you do use it, your victims will remain unconscious for as long as you possess their powers. The length of this transfer of powers is proportional to the length of the physical contact. Occasionally, the will of a victim may subvert your own, making you a danger to your own teammates, or the thoughts of a victim may repulse you so strongly that you are temporarily unable to act.

Teleportation is the special ability of Nightcrawler. When you play the blue-furred mutant, you are able to transport yourself instantly from one point to another at will. The greater the distance, or the more weight you are carrying (other people, for example), the more difficult and dangerous the teleportation FEAT. You are reluctant to attempt to teleport to an unknown place for fear of trapping your body inside a solid substance. It hasn't happened to you yet, but you fear it would kill you.

Leadership is a skill Storm has developed over many years, under the tutelage of Professor Xavier. When you play Storm, you will frequently understand the strengths and weaknesses of your teammates better than they themselves do, and you will command their total respect. Your will to survive and your passion to protect others are indomitable, and you can find ways to succeed where others would give up.

ATTEMPTING A FEAT

Whenever the text calls for you to attempt a FEAT for a particular ability, roll one die and add the result to the number of points you have for that ability. For example, in order to attempt a Fighting FEAT, Wolverine would roll one die and add that to his Fighting ability of 8, unless he is fighting with his claws, in which case his Fighting ability would be 16. If Wolvie wanted to, he could add Karma to the die roll as well, as explained in the section "KARMA POINTS." A high die roll will generally mean that you are successful at a FEAT, while a low one usually means that you failed. Wolverine must take care when fighting with his claws, however, since a high die roll could mean he has cut his opponent fatally.

CHANGING CHARACTERS

Whenever you turn to a new section of text, you may find that you are suddenly playing a different member of the X-Men. You can tell which character you are playing by checking the letter in boldface type that follows the section number. For example, **16ON** would be Nightcrawler, **83R** is Rogue, **23S** Storm, **81W** Wolverine, and so forth. Be sure to check who you are playing before continuing so that you know exactly who you are supposed to be.

PLAYING WITHOUT DICE

Should you ever wish to play the adventure when dice are unavailable, there is a simple substitute that requires only pencil and paper. Simply write the numbers 1 through 6 on separate slips of paper and mix them up in a container. When a FEAT roll is called for, draw one of the slips, note the number, and place the slip back in the container. Each draw represents one roll of a die.

You, as the Uncanny X-Men, are now ready to face one of the most challenging adventures of your careers, as you try to avoid meeting AN X-CELLENT DEATH.
Turn to page 13 to begin your adventure. Good luck, and good choices!

"Be careful, *mein Freund*. She is their most dangerous player. We could lose all if she gets the advantage of us."

You note Nightcrawler's warning with a curt nod. Your fellow X-Man's analysis of your opponent is quite accurate, but you're dangerous, too.

"I'm the best at what I do," you always say, and you don't say it just to build your confidence. It just happens to be a fact. The woman opposite you holds a wooden bat, which you could shred into toothpicks with your adamantium claws, but that's not the way the game of baseball is played.

"Come on, Wolverine! Play ball!" Storm shouts from first base. She's just hit a single, but the other bases are empty. It's the bottom of the ninth, with two outs, and her team is losing by one run. The next batter, the one Nightcrawler warned you of, is Rogue, and with her superhuman strength, you might as well kiss the ball good-bye when she hits it.

"Don't rush me, woman!" you growl back at Storm, who has proven to be as formidable a baseball team captain as she is a leader of the X-Men. Even though she was robbed of her superhuman powers, she's a born leader and a real scrapper. To counter her shrewd line-up of batters, you must consider your strategy carefully.

Roberto Da Costa bats after Rogue, and you have no doubt you can strike the little twerp out. After all, he's only a New Mutant, the junior class at Professor Charles Xavier's School for Gifted Youngsters. Roberto is hot-headed and can be easily psyched out. But if Rogue gets an extra-base hit, Storm may score and the game will be tied. And if Rogue hits a homer, the game will be over and her team will have won. And you hate to lose.

Storm is affectionately tousling the hair of your first baseman, Rahne Sinclair, another New Mutant. You can see that Storm is trying to put the girl off-guard so that she can steal a base. Fortunately, Rahne's fellow student, your second baseman, Danielle Moonstar, is a tougher case. And your third baseman, the youngest

1W

13

X-Man, Kitty Pryde, has earned the nickname "the Executioner" for her ability to tag out people who reach her territory.

You take one last look at Rogue and Da Costa from the pitcher's mound. Make an Intuition FEAT by rolling one die and adding the result to your Intuition ability. If the result is 20 or less, turn to **81**. If it's 21 or more, turn to **119**.

2S The pistol seems to have no effect whatsoever on the Sentinel. You continue firing, at the same time shouting for Wolverine to come to your aid. *He may be Rogue's only hope!* you think desperately.

Turn to **154**.

3W Out of the corner of your eye, you see that Rogue seems to be recovering from the poison, at least enough to throw herself back into the fray.

Turn to **189**.

4N You give the ninja sword a twirl, enjoying the feel of its balance. You'd like to take it with you, but you have no sheath to put it in. You roll the ninja over, intent on "borrowing" his sash for the purpose. To your horror, you discover there's very little of his body inside the clothes! Before your eyes, the rest of it vaporizes away!

"Wolverine!" you whisper in shock. "This man is disintegrating!"

"Yep," he answers matter-of-factly. "The Hand assassins do that when they die—and even when they become unconscious. Don't want any prisoners to be taken."

"These are the Hand? The same ninja assassins who tried to kill you in Japan? But why are they here?"

"Obviously, someone hired 'em to do a job here. . . . What's that?" he points to a weapon tucked inside the ninja's belt.

You lift it out. "A subsonic pistol. He must have taken it from one of the guards."

"Why would a ninja assassin need a subsonic pistol?" Wolverine muses, puzzled.

"For the same reason we do—to fight off the centis?" you guess.

"If that's true, it's good news for us."

"Yes," you agree. "That would mean that the centis are giving them trouble as well."

"I think it's time we reported back to Storm," Wolverine says.

You glance one last time at the shell of clothing that only minutes ago held a man. A shudder runs down your spine as you wonder what sort of fanatic would do such a thing to himself, or allow it to be done to him. "*Ja*. Let's go!" you reply.

You teleport back to the clearing in front of the research base and start toward the entrance. No invisible field blocks your way.

"They've shut off the mass wall," you note.

"Let's hope it's because they saw us coming and not because it collapsed," Wolverine mutters.

Suddenly, your fellow X-Man whirls around, sensing some danger. Behind you, a ninja springs out of the darkness. Wolverine is ready to leap back into battle, but you grab his arm and hold him back.

With amusement, you watch the ninja bang into the mass wall and fall back.

"I think they have the mass wall back up."

"I think you're right," Wolverine agrees, grinning.

The door to the base slides open, and Storm and Mrs. Taggert usher you inside quickly.

"Nice timing!" Wolverine says.

"That is Dr. Kirsch's doing," Storm explains. "I am glad you are both back safely. What was that thing that came at you?"

Quickly, you fill the X-Men leader in on your discovery of the Hand's presence on the island.

"This gets worse and worse!" Storm mutters. "Kurt,

I want you to explore the base thoroughly with Mrs. Taggert. We may need you to play the shell game with these people."

"The shell game? What's that supposed to mean?" Leona Taggert asks curiously.

"A defensive maneuver," Storm explains. "You are all peas, and the rooms of this base are the shells. Nightcrawler will teleport you around to different rooms, making it difficult for the enemy to find you, should they breach the mass field. Nightcrawler, when you've finished, report to the command center. Wolverine, come with me."

You and Mrs. Taggert watch Storm lead Wolverine down the corridor. You marvel at how efficiently she has taken charge of the situation.

Turn to **46**.

5S "All right!" Rogue cheers. "We've got the little suckers on the run!"

"Unfortunately," you reply, "they've fled in the direction we're going. We may be ambushed again."

Cautiously, your team climbs up the hill. There, in the last rays of the sunlight, you can just make out the skeletal ruins of three barracks buildings. A fourth building stands miraculously untouched by the fire that destroyed everything else. Beside a door on the building are the stenciled letters "HQ."

"This must be our destination," you note grimly.

As you and your companions approach the door, it slides open, and a woman in army overalls leaps out, aiming a gun right at you!

Before you can react, the gun makes a horrible grating noise, and there is a loud crashing sound behind you.

Unharmed by the woman's weapon, you whirl around to discover her true target—another sphere, which now lies on the ground behind you.

"Inside, quick!" the woman orders. "Before it gets any darker!"

Not sure what you have to fear from the darkness but perfectly willing to take cover, you herd your team through the door. Inside, the woman pushes a button, and the door slides closed with an electronic *swish*. Then, into an intercom by the control panel, she orders, "Screen up!"

Finally, your hostess turns to greet you. "Welcome to what's left of Obar Island. I'm Jesse." You reach out for her extended hand, and she gives you a firm, quick handshake.

You note that Jesse is about your height and build, with short, brown hair and freckles. In her late twenties or early thirties, she exudes health and confidence, which make her seem much more attractive than a photograph of her could possibly capture.

"You're wearing an army uniform," Kurt notes. "This was an army installation, then?"

"What? This old thing?" Jesse laughs. "Just something I threw on. This is no army base, pal. This is Nerd Paradise. Follow me. The others will be dying to meet you."

Turn to **94**.

6R

"Ah belong to me!" you cry out, resisting with all your strength the feeling that you have lost control of yourself. "Ah believe in life, not death!"

When you finally manage to focus your eyes on the moonlit woods again, Wolverine is beside you with his arms around you. Your face is covered with tears.

"Are you all right?" he whispers.

"Yeah. Just frightened. There's . . . something else in his head. Oh, Logan, it was just awful!"

"I shouldn't have let you try it," Wolverine says, obviously angry at himself.

"No, really, ah'm okay. And ah found out what we need to know," you insist.

Add 2 to your Karma Pool for fighting down the ninja's will and learning what you needed to know. Then turn to **186**.

You shoot one foot out toward the ninja's head, **7S**
but he ducks in the nick of time. In retaliation, he
slashes at your leg with his sword. Your quick movement protects you from the full brunt of his attack, but
the blade slices through your leather pants and into
your flesh. The wound is only superficial, but it starts
to burn immediately. Then your leg goes numb.

His blade is poisoned! you realize as you collapse to the
ground. The ninja lunges toward you for a final blow,
but he crumples to the ground before he succeeds. Wolverine stands behind the assassin, still holding the
rock he used to clobber your enemy on the head.

Your companion kneels beside you. "Storm? Hang in
there, darlin'. I'll get you back inside."

"Rogue!" you whisper hoarsely. "Take care of her
first!"

"I'll take care of you both," Wolverine replies. "Don't
worry about a thing." Even though Wolverine is
wounded, you know he will not give up trying to protect you. As you begin to pass out from the poison, you
only hope your friend will not die himself because of his
efforts. Your adventure is over.

"Something's wrong," you whisper to Storm, **8W**
"but I can't make out exactly what."

"I feel it, too," your team leader replies. "Something
is hiding near this hill. Perhaps—"

Whatever Storm was about to suggest is cut off suddenly as a dark horde of at least twenty robotlike
spheres swoops down upon you and your companions.

Pencil-thin blue rays of energy slice through your
group. As it strikes, each beam feels like a molten-hot
bullet ripping through you, even though your clothing
and skin remain undamaged. Rogue seems oblivious to
the beams, but you, Storm, and Nightcrawler must
each subtract 5 from your Health points.

You are searching for something to climb to reach the
airborne spheres, when Nightcrawler reaches out and
places a hand on your shoulder. Turn to **72**.

9R The metal ball smacks down into your palm like a pop fly in a baseball game.

"Rogue, give it to me, *Leibchen!*" Nightcrawler calls out, reaching for the missile.

You look into Kurt's haggard face and think, *He's worked so hard tonight. Is he really up to teleporting the ball away and getting back safely?*

If you decide to hand the missile to Nightcrawler, turn to **155**. If you think you'd better take care of the problem yourself, turn to **109**.

10R You decide you can't risk waiting for Wolverine to return. *Ah might as well get this over with,* you think. *But ah'm not touchin' this creep with my face.* You take a firm grip of your prisoner with one hand, yank off the glove on the other hand with your teeth, and touch your bare hand to the prisoner's.

Caught completely unaware, the ninja's mind flows effortlessly into your own, but the thoughts there are so repulsive you almost wish he could have resisted you.

Your mind fills with visions of uncountable bodies that you—no, that *he*—has killed mercilessly. His mind does not even seem to be his own. He thinks only of a master who owns his soul. You grow sickened by his lust for death.

With horror, you realize that the Hand assassin's body, without its consciousness, is beginning to dissolve! *S'pose he's trapped in me forever?* you think desperately. *What is Wolverine going to think?*

Darkness envelops you. You must make a Power Absorption FEAT by rolling one die and adding the result to your Power Absorption ability. If the total is 12 or less, turn to **86**. If it is 13 or more, turn to **143**.

11R "Once we get farther down this slope," Storm says, "the cover of darkness will work just as well for us as it does for the Hand."

You nod in agreement, glad the team is staying

together. Things always seem to go better when you work as a team.

Wolverine and Storm both creep down the path stealthily. You fly a few feet overhead, circling about them slowly, making no more noise than the wind.

"The Hand are still followin'. They're going to corner us if we don't do something, 'Roro," Wolverine says with concern.

"Patience, friend," Storm whispers. "I'm getting a signal now."

The frequency of the blinking light on the centi-scan steadily increases as Ororo leads you down the slope.

"There's an opening ahead," Wolverine whispers, pointing out a dark space in the rocks. "I hear centis! They're comin' out!"

As you land beside your companions, Wolverine draws his subsonic pistol, but Storm holds his arm down. "Wait a moment!" she orders, pulling both of you down into a crouch at her side.

At least twenty centis buzz out of the hillside, apparently fully charged with power. They hover for a moment only a few yards from you, then continue up the slope.

Above, you hear a cry, and you see the centis firing their weapons. Suddenly, one of them explodes.

"Who are they attackin'?" you wonder aloud.

"The ninjas, I believe," Storm answers. "Against the warm, dark ground, neither their infrared vision nor their regular sight could make us out, so they attacked the next available target."

"But aren't they all fightin' for the same thing?" you whisper.

"Perhaps not," Storm replies. "Or perhaps the centis have inherited one of their larger cousins' worst traits."

"What's that?" you ask.

"Betrayal," Wolverine says, grinning. Turn to **83**.

Wolverine and Roberto have been feuding for **125** as long as you can remember, but you don't really know what to do about it. "Robbie, keep calm," you order. "Don't let Logan get to you. It's just a game." Da Costa does not answer. He just continues to scowl at Wolverine.

You sigh with resignation. At a loss for anything else to say, you simply urge, "Go get 'im, kid!"

"Don't worry. I will show him," Da Costa replies as you head back to second base.

Wolverine throws the first two pitches well inside. You know how annoying it is to have the ball come so close to your body, certain that it's going to hit you, but Wolverine's aggressive playing style has never bothered you. Roberto, however, who's convinced that Wolverine is out to get him personally, blows his cool completely. A few fast balls later, he has struck out. The game is over. A feeling of dissatisfaction sweeps over you, but it has more to do with the problem of Roberto and Wolverine than with losing this ballgame.

Determined to hide your feelings, you approach the pitcher's mound to shake Logan's hand. "Congratulations," you say sincerely.

"Thanks, Ororo. You didn't do too bad yourself," Wolverine replies.

"However, now I must go salve some wounded egos," you continue. "Excuse me." You pat each of your teammates on the back in turn. There's Sam Guthrie, another New Mutant; Roberto; Rogue; and Peter Rasputin, also known as Colossus. "We played a good game. Next time we'll beat them for sure," you say, trying to sound convincing.

From the corner of your eye, you see Nightcrawler patting Wolverine on the back. Turn to **150**.

13R Just as you feel the missile start to explode, you bend over it and shield it with your body! The force of the blast sends you hurtling into the cold, dark water. *Oh, mama!* you think. *Ah've never hurt so much in mah whole life!*

You hear screaming, and then the voice of Storm, giving orders to haul you out of the water. You feel yourself yanked into the boat. You want to tell Storm you'll be fine, just as soon as you get back home for a little rest, but no words come to your lips. *Ah sure hope the rest of the trip is uneventful,* you think as your thoughts fade into darkness. Your adventure is over.

Back in the control center, you find it hard to **14N** sit still as you wonder what Wolverine and Rogue will discover outside. Just then, Jesse returns from escorting your teammates to the door of the mass wall. She looks somber.

"Is something wrong?" Michael asks.

"No. What could be wrong?" Jesse says weakly.

Dr. Craig glances up from the monitors and harumphs derisively. "Even I can see you are not your usual buoyant self, Dr. Kirsch."

Jesse shrugs. "I may as well tell you. We found a shuriken buried in the door. It could only have gotten there between the time I closed the door and raised the mass wall. That was all of five seconds. Wolverine says someone must be watching the building."

"Ninjas!" Michael cheers. "Neat!"

You feel less enthusiastic than Michael. *Why would ninja assassins be here?* you wonder.

"That might explain the shadows that Michael saw," Storm conjectures.

"Ninjas prefer working under the cover of darkness," you point out.

"Yes," Storm replies. "That's true. By day, the centis function well, with their solar rechargers, while ninjas prefer to operate at night. It is a curious coincidence, is it not?"

"*Ja*," you agree.

"Dr. Laughlin," Storm asks, "do you think someone could give Nightcrawler a tour of your facility?"

"Is it really necessary?" Dr. Laughlin asks. "Nothing personal, but most of our labs are top secret."

"I should see it," you tell him, "in case we need to play the shell game later."

"The shell game?" the director asks blankly.

"If your defenses are breached, you will be the pea and these rooms will be the shells. If I know the facility, I can teleport you and your associates from one place to another, making it more difficult for the enemy to find you."

"All of us? Won't that wear you out?" Jesse asks.

"Eventually," you admit, "but we can rely on Wolverine and Rogue to fight off the invaders."

"Why don't you let me handle the tour, Gerald?" Dr. Kirsch asks Dr. Laughlin.

"Can I come along?" Michael asks eagerly.

"Isn't it your bedtime, young man?" you ask.

"It certainly is," his mother replies.

"But I don't want to miss out if anything happens," Michael complains.

"I assure you that we will wake you when we need your help," Storm tells him.

Michael seems to sense that Storm means what she said, and he allows himself to be led from the room by his mother and Dr. Laughlin.

"Nightcrawler, report back to me within an hour," Storm orders. "I'll be right here, keeping an eye out for Wolverine and Rogue."

You follow Jesse from the control center, leaving Storm behind with Dr. Craig.

Once you are out in the corridor, you give Jesse a flirtatious wink. "Alone at last!" you say jokingly.

The female scientist smiles back at you. "You know, Michael really could have come with us. He's not that bad for a kid, and he knows this place better than I do."

"Perhaps," you reply, "but when I go for an evening stroll with a lovely lady, I do not like to share her company with younger men."

Jesse laughs. "I see. Well, maybe we'd better start at the top and work our way down."

"How about starting at the door where we entered?" you suggest.

"Good idea. This way."

Jesse motions toward another corridor. Turn to **161**.

Whatever it was the centi-bot used on you, **15W**
your body doesn't seem up to coping with it immediately. You don't feel any better or worse by resting. Turn to **129**.

You fire at the approaching light, wincing at **16N**
the grating noise made by your sonic pistol. Instantly, the centi acts confused. The robotic sphere fires several narrow blue rays at the walls as it spins around erratically, then explodes. Its remains clatter to the ground.

Rogue comes zooming down the corridor. She stops in front of the centi's shell, then looks toward you and says, "Well, ah can see you don't need any help!"

"No, *Fraulein*, but your company is greatly appreciated. Shall we stroll back and join Storm and Wolverine?"

Turn to **87**.

You advance toward the door of the base until **17W**
you can feel the mass wall. It doesn't give. "It figures that jerk Gyrich would be involved in this," you mutter, leaning up against the wall and pulling out a cigar.

"Oooh, ah'd love to get my hands on him!" Rogue declares hotly. It had been Rogue's powers that Gyrich had meant to destroy when he'd accidentally hit Storm with a neutralizing ray.

"Now, now," Nightcrawler says. "Let's not do anything to make the man any more paranoid than he already is."

"I know what I'd like to make him," you mutter as you light up your cigar. You have nothing but contempt for the government agent.

The wall behind you suddenly feels softer, and you stand upright to keep from falling backward. The four of you move toward the door, but it still doesn't open.

"Jesse's done her bit," Storm says. "Nightcrawler, teleport us into the control room, please."

Nightcrawler disappears with Storm and Rogue and

then returns for you. When you get there, all the members of the research team are gathered in the control room. Dr. Laughlin, Mrs. Taggert, and Michael are wrapped in their bathrobes, looking bleary-eyed. Red lights blink over the doors, and Klaxon bells sound over the public-address system. Jesse is seated at a control panel, oblivious to the noise around her.

"How did you get Gyrich to let us back in?" Nightcrawler asks her.

"I didn't," Jesse says. "I arranged a little diversion, a small laboratory explosion, to get him out of the room, then lowered the field again without his permission."

You hear a sudden scream from the corridor. The door to the control room slides open, and Gyrich steps into the room.

The members of the research team all freeze in horror, but you merely chuckle. Henry Peter Gyrich is covered with some sort of gooey green substance that drips from his body. Not even Storm can resist a smile.

"I also left a bucket of green slime perched over the lab door," Jesse whispers to Kurt. "I couldn't resist!"

You turn your attention from the spluttering government agent back to Storm, waiting to take your cue from her. Turn to **118**.

18N

You and Jesse teleport back to the command center to tell Storm what you've found. Wolverine and Rogue have not returned yet, but Storm is no longer alone with Dr. Craig. Two other men hover over the X-Men team leader. One of them is Dr. Andrews, and the other, you realize, is the much discussed Henry. It is not just any Henry. It is a Henry you know.

"Gyrich!" you snarl, for the self-appointed security chief of Obar Island is none other than Henry Peter Gyrich. Gyrich is known to be a member of the National Security Council, a headache to super heroes everywhere, but especially an enemy to mutants. He is the man responsible for Storm's loss of her mutant powers. He had meant to take away Rogue's powers, but he has never displayed any regret that he hit Storm by accident. If he had his way, mutants would be tagged, even given radio collars like wild bears—all mutants, whether they'd committed any crime or not.

Gyrich spins about, glaring daggers at you. Storm acts completely unperturbed by Gyrich's and Andrews's hostility. Dr. Craig is, as always, glued to the monitors, remaining completely detached from the scene. Gyrich chooses to address Jesse first. "Dr. Kirsch, you should consider yourself on report for disobeying my order by lowering the mass field and letting someone inside this facility."

"If it weren't for me, the mass field would have collapsed a long time ago," Jesse snaps back.

"I won't stand for insubordination, Dr. Kirsch. I'll see you never work again," Gyrich retorts.

"Fine! Why don't you just keep the mass field up?" Jesse removes a screwdriver and a pocket calculator from her pockets and holds them out toward the security advisor.

"You will continue in your present position or I'll have you court-martialed!"

"Gee, Henry," Jesse replies breathily, "why don't you just take out that big, shiny .45 bulging in your jacket and shoot me with it?"

Knowing Gyrich, you're not surprised when he does pull out his gun, but he aims it at you and Storm, not Jesse. "You mutants are under arrest for trespassing."

"Storm," you whisper, "I would really like to punch this guy."

"I do not recommend it, Kurt," Storm whispers back sternly. "I understand how you feel, however."

You move between Jesse and Gyrich. "If you are quite through acting like an unchivalrous baboon, Gyrich," you say, "we have a mysterious underground passage that requires our attention."

"I forbid you to view any more of this base!" Gyrich huffs. "If you resist arrest, I'll be forced to add espionage and sabotage to the charge of trespassing."

"I've listened to enough of this nonsense," you

declare. "We came here to help you!"

"We don't need your kind of help, mutant scum!" Gyrich spits.

If you decide to punch Gyrich, turn to **114**. If you think you'd better just ignore this insulting jerk, turn to **47**.

19R The moment Storm nods her approval of the mission, you run to tell the other members of the team, but you find no one left at the school. They all must have gone into town to quench their thirst after the ball game, you finally decide. It is just the four of you—Storm, Nightcrawler, Wolverine, and yourself—who set out from Spuyten Cove in the small motorboat, the *Lilandra*.

It's still early enough in the spring for the lake's surface to be nearly deserted. You spot a few kids fishing along the shoreline, but no boats beside your own disturb the surface of the water. Storm sends you ahead to scout for any water patrol boats that might be blocking your route to the island.

Exulting in the thrill of flight, you rise out of the boat and soar overhead, high enough to be mistaken for a bird if you are seen at all. Flying through the air, you feel at peace with the world. Innumerable times, you have been plagued with guilt over stealing Ms. Marvel's powers and consciousness and wished you could give them back—all the memories, the strength, the invulnerability, and the seventh sense. But to part with this gift of flying would be impossibly difficult.

Ah could stay up here forever! you think. But there is work to be done, so you return to the boat and report that there are no other craft on the lake at all.

"How odd," Storm murmurs. As you pass the first warning buoy, posted with a "NO TRESPASSING" notice, you spot a large, dark object floating in the water.

"It looks like a body!" you whisper.

"Why don't you check it out, Rogue?" Storm suggests.

You skim low over the water toward the shape. It is indeed a corpse, that of a man in army uniform. A creepy feeling shudders along your spine, but you dutifully pluck at the dead man's shirt and, getting a good grasp on it, haul the corpse back toward the boat.

Suddenly you feel as though you've slammed into a brick wall. You splash backward into the water, losing hold of your burden. Nightcrawler maneuvers the *Lilandra* up beside you.

"Are you all right?" Storm asks anxiously.

"Ah'm fine, but somethin' hit me. Did you see what it was?"

"There's nothing around," Wolverine says, reaching out to pull you back into the boat.

Nightcrawler begins circling the boat around closer to the corpse. You hear a thunk and the boat rocks sickeningly.

"We must have hit something," Nightcrawler says. "Perhaps a branch."

"Wait a minute, guys. There's somethin' fishy here," you insist. You fly away from the boat, keeping your hands in front of you. A few yards away, you hit what feels like a smooth rock wall.

"It's some sort o' force field," you cry out, flying upward and feeling along the invisible surface. A few hundred feet up, the wall curves inward. You plunge down into the water, exploring the range of the barrier. It goes all the way down to the lake bottom and into the muck.

At the limits of your breath, you swim to the surface and emerge from the water. Landing carefully in the boat, you accept a towel from Storm.

You tell the others what you've discovered as you dry yourself off. "It goes all the way down. Prob'ly curves over the whole island up above."

"But we didn't hit anything while we were going toward the island," Nightcrawler protests. "Only when we tried to move away."

"It's probably a one-way barrier to keep people from gettin' off the island," Wolverine guesses. "Now I've *gotta* see what's going on out on that rock!"

Using a boat hook, Storm hauls the soldier's body aboard. The dead man appears to have been stabbed.

"Whoever did this is undoubtedly on the island," Storm surmises. "Kurt, before we go any farther, check to the near shore and back."

Without hesitation, Nightcrawler vanishes in a small explosion, leaving a puff of foul-smelling smoke behind. A few seconds later, he reappears in the same theatrical way, but he looks somewhat drained.

"Are you all right? What happened?" you ask.

Kurt shrugs his shoulders. "I don't know exactly. It was suddenly as if the shore were a hundred miles away. I couldn't make it. I had to turn back."

"I guess we have no choice but to go forward," Storm says reluctantly. A minute later, the boat reaches Obar Island's dock—a solid, new construction, sheltering four powerboats with U.S. Army identification numbers on them and a small sailboat. The shadows are lengthening considerably as you debark with your companions. The smell of smoke is heavy all around you, and you can hear the roar and crackle of a fire somewhere in the distance.

Just as you step onto the path into the forest, Wolverine cries out, "Rogue! Look out!" and shoves you to the ground as a horrible, buzzing sphere about the size of a volleyball swoops down over your head!

You spin around to find the sphere attached to Wolverine's wrists by steel tendrils, like space-age handcuffs.

Wolverine turns pale and cries out in pain. "It's tryin' to cut off my wrists!"

Ah've gotta get this thing off of Wolvie! you think as you grab the sphere to crush it.

Make a Strength FEAT by rolling one die and adding the result to your Strength ability. If the sum is 16 or more, turn to **163**. If it is 14 or 15, turn to **56**. If it is 13 or less, turn to **38**.

You gash deep into the Sentinel's legs. Metal **20W** bends under the strain of the giant's weight, then snaps. The Sentinel crashes to the ground, and Rogue's body rolls from its grasp.

You leap onto the Sentinel's torso and climb toward the creature's throat. All the while it shouts, "This unit down! Mutant poses formidable threat to this unit!"

Make an Intuition FEAT by rolling one die and adding the result to your Intuition ability. If the total is 19 or less, turn to **37**. If it is 20 or more, turn to **177**.

21N You could be content to sit here, watching Wolverine in action, as though he were the hero of some action movie. But you are rudely reminded that this is reality when you catch sight of a third ninja pulling on a bow string, its arrow aimed at your friend.

Teleporting to the archer's side, you tap him on the shoulder. Although he is wearing a mask, you can still detect the startled look in his eyes. Quickly, you teleport him about the beach several times, an experience that generally leaves the uninitiated stunned or unconscious. It tends to wear you out a little, too.

Finally you let go of the ninja, but unfortunately, he shows no signs of losing consciousness. Instead, he turns on you with a drawn sword.

"Um . . . as you can see, I am unarmed," you say, crouching defensively. The ninja sneers and jabs at you with his weapon.

Make an Agility FEAT by rolling one die and adding the result to your Agility ability. If the total is 13 or less, turn to **122**. If it is 14 or more, turn to **42**.

22R The branch you grasp bends under your weight, but it holds. You hang above the ground for a moment, then pull yourself up, working your way into the fork of the tree. You reach down carefully to touch the man bound to the trunk.

Oh, gosh! you say, shuddering and drawing your hand back quickly. The man's body is cold. You realize he's been dead for some time.

You can see that there is a wire twisted around a lock of his hair. The other end of the wire leads off into the woods. Someone must have tugged on the wire to make it look as though the corpse's head moved.

"These Hand people are really sick!" you mutter as Wolverine enters the clearing cautiously.

"Careful!" you whisper. "There's a booby trap laid around this tree. The guy is dead."

Wolverine nods. "I know. I could smell him and the booby trap—it's a napalm bomb. If you're finished playin' Shanna the She-Devil, we can move on," he whispers back.

You fly down to the ground, careful to avoid landing anywhere near the booby trap, and follow Wolverine from the clearing. Turn to **178**.

Jesse fixes Dr. Andrews with a withering glare. **23S** "Jonathan, these are the X-Men. They do not murder people. They're heroes. They've come to rescue us."

"They're outlaw mutants!" Dr. Andrews argues. "They're responsible for unimaginable destruction!"

"So's the U.S. Air Force," Jesse sniffs, "but that's never stopped you from designing weaponry for them."

"I appreciate the vote of confidence," you say to Jesse. "It is true that our purpose in coming here was to offer what assistance we could, but what makes you so certain that Dr. Andrews isn't correct?"

"I was in Tokyo a few years back. I watched you guys in action when you saved that city from that huge green dragon. As far as I'm concerned, actions speak louder than—well, even louder than old Jonathan here."

You smile, recalling that battle. It was one of your last before your powers were destroyed. Brave people died in that catastrophe, but in the end, after the monster had fled, presumably back to its own world, the Japanese government had thanked you. Gratitude was something your team wasn't used to receiving—it certainly rarely came from the U. S. government, which had more reasons to thank you than it would ever know.

"These shadows that you saw—what did they do?" you ask Michael.

"They sneaked into the generator building," Michael replies. "A few minutes later—*kablooey!*"

"That's what started the fire," Dr. Laughlin says. "The mass field kept burning trees from falling on top of this building, but the heat almost roasted us. And we were in the dark for some time."

"But you have power now," you note, indicating all the lighted control panels around you.

"There's an experimental generator in the basement, meant originally just for the mass field," Jesse explains.

"How long will it last? Perhaps you should be conserving your energy," you suggest.

"The power will last as long as it needs to," Jesse says.

"Jesse just kicks the generator and it keeps running," Michael adds with a giggle.

"That so?" Rogue laughs.

"Steel-toed boots," says Jesse. "Got to know how to talk to these machines. If we were to search outside, you could let us back in when we returned."

"Yes," Dr. Laughlin agrees.

"You can't lower the field again!" Dr. Andrews argues.

"Jonathan, please," Dr. Laughlin sighs, "I am still the director here."

"Henry will not allow it."

"Better run and tell Henry quick, Jonathan," Jesse teases.

"I'll do precisely that!" Dr. Andrews declares as he scurries from the room.

"Thomas? Do you have any objections?" Dr. Laughlin asks.

"You know that I do not involve myself in policy," Dr. Craig replies. "I'm a scientist, not a politician."

"It's your life at stake as well as ours," Dr. Laughlin points out.

Dr. Craig shrugs.

"Don't worry about Thomas, Gerald," Jesse jokes. "He'll be standing at the pearly gates arguing with St. Peter that he can't possibly be dead, and if old Pete has any sense, he'll send him back to Earth."

"Can you loan us one of those subsonic pistols?" you ask Jesse.

"Sure. Take this. I'll just whip up another one," Jesse

answers, handing her weapon over to you.

From the corner of the room, Michael's mother asks meekly, "You aren't *all* going to leave us, are you?"

"You'll be safe behind the field, Mrs. Taggert," you reply.

"But Dr. Kirsch *is* having trouble with the mass field," the woman argues.

You look over at Jesse. She stares up at the ceiling, as though reluctant to meet your gaze. "We have plenty of power, but the field is controlled by the computer, and there are some bugs in the program," she admits.

"I'll have to leave someone here," you decide. "I think, Wolverine, you should be one of those who investigates. I'll stay behind."

To yourself you think, *This way I won't be a hindrance to Logan, with only my human skills to rely on.* But you also feel that you will be the most competent at convincing Henry, whoever he is, of the need to lower the shield to let your teammates back in.

Who should I send with Wolverine, and who should I keep here with me? you ask yourself. "I may need Rogue's superior strength if the generator collapses, and Wolverine and Nightcrawler work well together. On the other hand, Rogue would be much safer outside than Kurt, and Kurt, like me, is much better at dealing with people.

If you decide to send Rogue with Wolverine and keep Nightcrawler at the base with you, turn to **199**. If you want to keep Rogue with you and send Nightcrawler outside with Wolverine, turn to **39**.

24N

You grab one miniature robot between your feet and one with your tail, but the third slips out from between your hands and fires at you before you can teleport away. Hit at close range on the forehead by one of the blue beams, you feel as though your head is on fire!

Unable to concentrate, you crash to the ground and lose your grip on the two robots. Immediately they begin firing at you with the thin blue beams.

In agony, you lift your head, only to see Rogue crash to the ground nearby. Then you pass out from the pain, hoping that Storm and Wolverine can carry on where you have failed. Your adventure has ended.

25N The centi closes in relentlessly. You shield Storm's body with your own.

"I feel very naked standing here," you whisper.

"And the lock is very rusty," Storm mutters. "It will take a few moments more."

Suddenly, the centi unleashes a bolt of blue light right at your shoulder, sending excruciating pain down your arm and back, but you bear the pain without a sound. Subtract 1 from your Health points and turn to **164**.

26W You were just thinking that you were finally getting the upper hand when Rogue's shout makes you aware of Michael's presence. Now you have the added problem of freeing the boy.

As you leap from the Sentinel's chest to the hand that clutches Michael, the Sentinel's voice booms out, "This mutant must be exterminated first!"

You don't have time to wonder whether the Sentinel's mutant sensors are faulty or what. All you can think of is freeing Michael.

You slash savagely at the Sentinel's wrist with your claws. Make a Fighting FEAT roll and add the result to your Fighting With Claws ability. If the total is 19 or less, turn to **32**. If it is 20 or more, turn to **191**.

You slash at your metal attackers with a speed **27W** that is hard for the eye to follow. Sparks fly as your claws strike against the steel casings of the miniature robots.

These things are gonna be sorry they ever hatched, you vow to yourself, but a more serious consideration directs your actions. If they fly past you, Rogue can probably withstand their attacks, and Nightcrawler can teleport away, but Storm, without her super powers, will be a sitting duck. Turn to **187**.

Before you immerse yourself in the details of **28S** the centi-tracking device, you send Rogue to the infirmary to get Nightcrawler.

"Don't let him try to convince you he's well enough to walk on his own," you insist. "Carry him."

"Yes'm, boss," Rogue says. She leaves the room to carry out your orders. Turn to **91**.

In your heart, you know that Jesse is right. **29N** The stakes in this game are too high to take any chances. Too many people are depending on you to get them out of this predicament. If anything happens to you, the team will be severely weakened.

"Fair lady, you do well to remind me of my duty," you say grandly, bending over Jesse's hand and brushing your lips to her skin.

"It was nothing, really," Jesse replies, sounding just a little flustered.

"I shall whisk you back to Lady Storm, and we shall take counsel with her."

"Good idea," Jesse laughs as you take her in your arms to teleport the two of you back to the control room. Turn to **18**.

As you relax, you both feel and see your **30W** miraculous healing powers begin to work. The bruises on your flesh disappear before your eyes, and your muscles and joints no longer ache. You may add 2 more points to your Health, then turn to **129**.

31S It's vital that you make the government agent realize he has more to fear from the Hand than from the X-Men. The lives of all the people you came here to rescue are at stake!

"Mr. Gyrich," you say with a sigh, "you cannot hide here forever behind the mass field. It may collapse anyway, and the Hand will swarm inside. They've already killed your security guards. We are simply trying to help you escape them."

"I don't need any help from you, mutant!" Gyrich retorts. "We're staying here.

Dr. Laughlin shakes his head slowly. Then his jaw sets determinedly. From somewhere inside himself, the base director finds the courage to countermand the government agent's orders.

"Jesse, lower both mass fields," he says quietly.

"No!" Gyrich screams. "You can't do that! They'll escape!"

"You are pathetic, Gyrich," Rogue snaps. "People's lives are at stake, and all you can think about is arrestin' us for tryin' to help you."

Dr. Laughlin says, "I think, Henry, that the strain of keeping us all safe these past several days has begun to wear you down. It's time for us to leave. Dr. Andrews and Craig will help you destroy the security files. We are abandoning this base."

Gyrich stares daggers at the X-Men. "You've turned them against me, but you won't be so lucky when we meet again!" he threatens.

"Gyrich, shugah, we're never lucky when we meet you," Rogue replies. Turn to **102**.

32W Your first slash doesn't go deep enough to damage the Sentinel's hand controls. Michael shrieks with pain as the monster continues to squeeze his helpless form. Angrily, you slash again. This time you cut right through the monster's wrist, and its fingers uncurl.

Nightcrawler teleports to your side. "I will see to the boy!" he says. "You take care of this killer!"

In a berserker rage, you turn to hack at the huge Sentinel. Rogue charges the creature, bashing in its face plate so you can get at the components in its head.

Not until the Sentinel is absolutely still, smoking and sparking, does your fury diminish. Storm continues to pick off occasional centis that venture near your group, but most of the miniature robots seem confused by their leader's demise and spin about without purpose.

You look down at the small body lying in the Sentinel's hand. "How bad is he hurt?" you ask Kurt as he stands up, looking shaken.

"He is alive, but he is unconscious from the pain. That is probably best for now. I fear that his spine has been broken."

"Oh, mah lord!" Rogue whispers.

"Do you think you can get him to the mainland?" Storm asks Nightcrawler.

"*Ja*. I will see that he gets immediate medical attention," he assures her.

"We will evacuate the others before the Hand can get to them, then meet you at the hospital," the X-Men leader says.

Nightcrawler teleports away with Michael's body.

You and Rogue dig out the rest of the shaft started by the Sentinel, though with a much smaller diameter. While Rogue is bringing Storm up to join you outside in the night air, you discover that the mass wall has collapsed. *We'll have to hurry before the Hand figure it out,* you think.

You're ready to give Storm all the help in your power to get the members of the research team free of the island and protect them from the Hand, but there's one task you do not think you can help her with—telling Mrs. Taggert of her son's injury.

Remembering that the Sentinel called Michael a mutant, you wonder if it's true, and just how many more innocents, mutant or human, other Sentinels will victimize in the years to come. Your adventure has come to an unsatisfactory conclusion.

33N

"There is a large space beneath the floor. What else is down there, who knows?" you tell Storm.

"Very well," she says, flicking on the flashlight at her belt. "Let's go."

You teleport seven feet straight down and begin to fall immediately!

With one hand, your feet, and your tail, you scramble for a hold, but the walls of the vertical shaft are out of reach. Unable to halt your descent, you try to protect Storm from getting injured when you land.

Make an Agility FEAT by rolling one die and adding the result to your Agility ability. If the total is 11 or less, turn to **149**. If it is 12, turn to **69**. If it is 13 or more, turn to **200**.

34N

You are not certain what the blue rays are, but you are willing to bet they'll hurt. You twist and gyrate your body, dodging out of the way of the beams of light, but there are just too many of them.

"Aaaach!" you cry out in pain as one of the rays strikes your shoulder. There is no hole in your costume or flesh, but you feel as if you've been shot at with a small lightning bolt. Quickly, you teleport to the battle's flank, turning to see that Rogue has flown into the swarm of creatures, unaffected by their attacks.

Storm cannot maneuver as quickly. Though she makes no sound, you can see your team leader's slender frame shudder each time a beam of light strikes her. Subtract 2 from your Health points and 4 from Storm's Health points. In the moment's respite that your retreat has brought you, you attempt a quick analysis of the creatures' attack. Turn to **60**.

35W

You and Nightcrawler creep along the path more silently than most wild creatures could. *I wish this Mikey kid had seen somethin' more than just shadows. We'd have a better idea of what to do if we knew what we're up against,* you think.

From out of the darkness comes a whistling noise. You feel a piercing pain in your neck and one knee. Behind you, you hear Nightcrawler cry out from pain, but he reacts quickly. Reaching out, he grabs you and teleports both of you back to the edge of the beach.

You pull two shiny pieces of metal out of your body. Nightcrawler holds up a third, which struck him in the shoulder. They are razor-sharp and star-shaped, with six points each—shurikens, glinting silver in the moonlight, except where they are stained with your blood. Subtract 4 from your Health points. Subtract 2 from Nightcrawler's Health point total.

"Offhand, I'd say we have met the enemy," Kurt whispers, "and we are wounded."

"Ninjas. And I never caught a whiff of 'em. They must be overhead in the trees. Two can play at that. How 'bout the top of that sugar maple?" you suggest.

Kurt teleports the two of you into the branches above the path, and you sit very still for several minutes. Finally, your patience is rewarded by the appearance of two shadowy figures, which finally come close enough

for you to smell that they are men. You leap down to attack, catching one off guard.

Make a Fighting FEAT by rolling one die and adding the result to your Fighting Without Claws ability. If the total is 10 or less, turn to **171**. If it is 11 or more, turn to **190**.

36W "You'd better not, Rogue," you decide. "These birds are just too strange. There's no tellin' what might happen to you. We'll take him back to the base. Maybe Dr. Kirsch could mix us up some truth serum."

"You're the boss," Rogue sighs. You can sense that she's torn between disappointment and relief. Using her power thrills her, but it also frightens her.

Suddenly, the prisoner Rogue holds goes limp in her arms.

"Be that way," Rogue says, eyeing the ninja. "I'll just carry you." She tucks him under one arm as if he were a sack of flour.

You can detect the subtle differences between a man who is relaxed and a man who has just died. A hint of poison makes your nostrils flare.

"I'm afraid he's dead," you tell Rogue.

"What?" your partner gasps, holding the man up to see for herself.

"He just poisoned himself. Must've been one of his own shurikens," you explain. "He couldn't risk being drugged and interrogated."

You notice that Rogue shivers slightly. You realize it isn't from the cold, but you decide to get something to cover her tattered costume. Turn to **117**.

37W You use your claws to keep yourself from slipping on the slick metal surface of the Sentinel, then step onto a circular grid on its chest. You hear something click inside the metallic monster. With no further warning, you are bathed in a molten red light by a beam that shoots out at you from the grid. You are lifted high into the air by the beam and out over the hillside.

You land hard, some distance away. Your flesh and hair are both badly singed. Subtract 4 from your Health points.

As injured as you are, you try to rise immediately, knowing Storm will need your help, but you collapse, unable to rise. "Sorry, Storm," you mutter. "It's up to you now, boss!" Turn to **53**.

38W You watch as Rogue begins to dent both sides of the metal object attacking you. In retaliation, the thing sends out a bright beam of light straight into your teammate's eyes. Instinctively, she raises her hands to shield her eyes, letting go of the sphere.

You feel a sudden prick on your arm. The sphere has stabbed you with a miniature hypodermic! You can sense the poison coursing through your veins. You must subtract 4 from your Health points.

With a *snikt!*, you unsheathe the long, deadly claws implanted in your hands, but your effort is futile since you cannot twist around to slash at your bindings. The poison is causing your muscles and joints to ache. You hope that your mutant ability to resist alien chemicals will neutralize it quickly.

Make a Fast Healing FEAT by rolling one die and adding the result to your Fast Healing ability. If the total is 23 or less, turn to **103**. If it is 24 or more, turn to **173**.

39R "I think Rogue had better stay here with me, just in case I need her later," Storm says. "Nightcrawler and Wolverine, you take a look around outside."

You give a small sigh and resign yourself to Storm's orders. You like Storm's company, but the prospects for action inside the research base seem rather slim.

"You are certain that the mass wall around the building will not prevent us from getting out?" Kurt asks.

"You won't even notice it, unless you try to come back through it," Dr. Laughlin assures him.

"I'll escort you back to the outer door," Jesse offers helpfully.

"No need, *Fraulein*," Nightcrawler says, smiling.

"You might get lost," Jesse warns.

Wolverine laughs. "The elf never gets lost, sweetheart. Why don't we start at that beach we saw when we came here?" he suggests.

"*Ja*," Nightcrawler agrees. "Sounds good."

"Be seein' ya," Wolverine says and winks at Michael. Nightcrawler lays his hands on Wolverine's shoulders and with a loud *bamf*, the two men teleport away.

"Far out!" Michael breathes.

"Perhaps you have a map of this installation that I could study," Storm suggests.

"You can call up the maps on the computer," Dr. Laughlin explains.

"I'll show her how," Mrs. Taggert volunteers. "You've been on watch for ten hours now, Gerald. Why don't you get some rest?"

"Thank you, Leona," Dr. Laughlin replies. "I think I'll do just that."

Yawning, the director leaves the command center. Mrs. Taggert offers Storm a chair at a computer terminal, but you aren't very interested in maps.

"Maybe ah could help you whip up some more of those sonic pistols," you suggest to Jesse.

"A woman of action, eh?" Jesse teases. "I have to run down and check on the mass field again. Michael, why don't you take Rogue down to the sound lab and show her how we build the subsonic pistols? I'll join you as soon as I can."

"Is that okay with you, boss?" you ask Storm, who is studying the graphics screen before her with intense concentration.

"Fine, Rogue," she says without looking up.

You follow Michael and Jesse out of the command center. At a branch of the corridors, the female scientist parts from your company. Behind you, she calls out, "Have fun!"

Turn to **141**.

45

40W *She looks like Rogue and smells like Rogue,* you reason, *but her body language is all wrong, and her Southern accent is gone.*

In a flash, you realize that the ninja's will is now in control of the young mutant's body.

Knowing you have only one chance to help Rogue regain control of her body, you leap at her before the Hand assassin who controls her can react. Turn to **44**.

41W As you stride alongside Storm, you begin to feel uneasy. Even with your instinctive sense of direction, you're not sure that you could find your way back.

"Flamin' place must be bigger on the inside than it is on the outside," you mutter.

Jesse stops in her tracks. "Do you really think so? That's what Michael and I think, too, but Thomas and Jonathan say that's impossible. Greg, of course, stays perfectly neutral on the subject. Part of the complex is underground. I think maybe we're in that part."

Storm nods and whispers, "It feels as though we are underground."

You remember that Storm is claustrophobic, though she can usually manage to keep her fear under control. You wonder if she's struggling with it now.

"You sure you aren't leading us around in circles?" you ask Jesse.

"Oh, quite. As a matter of fact, here we are now." Jesse opens a door and leads you into a large control room.

The room looks like an airport control tower without windows, full of computer control panels and LED screens. Or maybe it's more like a miniature NORAD, the North American Air Defense Command headquarters sheltered in the Rocky Mountains. You've been there, and the only difference is that this room isn't full of uniformed soldiers. You see only five people here, all dressed in civilian clothing—three men, another woman, and a boy not more than ten years old.

"Hey, guys! company!" Jesse calls out. Five curious faces turn in your direction. One of the men gasps. "How did they get past the shield?"

"Oh, Jonathan, calm down," Jesse says with a laugh. "Obviously, I invited them in. Can't have them wandering about at night. It's dangerous out there."

"Are you crazy?" Jonathan shouts. "Henry told us not to lower the shield for any reason."

"Henry can go brush his teeth with a light-sabre, for all I care," Jesse replies with a sniff.

Jonathan bristles. "Wait a minute. You couldn't have lowered the shield. The controls are all in here. Unless—" Jonathan looks at the boy, Michael, who remains seated very quietly at one of the control panels, looking innocently up at the ceiling.

"Michael?" Jonathan calls in a derisive tone as he heads menacingly toward the boy.

Michael bolts past Jonathan and hides behind Jesse. Tired of being ignored, you step in front of Jonathan before he can reach the two of them.

"You make a habit of threatening little kids, Mac?" you growl. Jonathan, more than six feet tall, towers over your short frame.

"Out of my way, mister!" he orders you.

"*Your* way?" you ask challengingly. "You got a deed for this piece of floor, pal?"

Just as the man before you tenses his muscles, preparing to push you, you unsheathe your claws with a *snikt*" and hold one fist up to his chin so he can see just what he's up against. Turn to **168**.

42N

You leap agilely to one side, avoiding your enemy's thrust. He hisses angrily.

"You know, this isn't very chivalrous of you," you say, resuming your defensive crouch.

The ninja brings his sword up high, apparently intent on slicing through your brains.

With a flick of your tail, you send a cloud of sand into the assassin's eyes. He backs off, swinging his weapon wildly, blinking furiously.

Immediately, you teleport behind him, sending him tumbling over you into the water with a loud splash.

"If you insist, we will fight dirty then, *ja?*" you taunt as you pounce on him and pound him with your fists. Stunned, the ninja's muscles go limp, and he loses his grip on his sword.

You drag his body from the water and retrieve the ninja's sword. At a sound from the trees, you whirl around, blade held ready, but you lower it with a sigh of relief when you see it is only Wolverine.

Turn to **4**.

43R

"I think we've been followed here," Wolverine whispers.

"By Gyrich?" you ask.

Wolverine shakes his head from side to side, meanwhile listening and sniffing the air. "Nope. It's the kid, Mikey. He's somewhere in the passage up above."

"Nightcrawler!" Storm whispers. "Get him back safely to his mother and return here pronto!"

"Yes'm." Kurt teleports away.

The rest of you have no time to wait for the blue mutant's return, however, for suddenly the Sentinel raises its hands to the ceiling, and a searing red ray shoots out of its palms. The cavern shakes about you, and chunks of the walls and ceiling shower over your heads. Over the Sentinel's head, a vertical shaft begins to take shape.

"We must stop him!" Storm orders. "The mass wall cannot protect the base from an earthquake!"

You are ready to fly at the Sentinel when Storm grabs your shirt. "Wait here for Nightcrawler, Rogue," she orders. "Wolverine, I'll cover you. Go!"

Wolverine lunges toward the Sentinel. Storm follows, wielding the sonic pistol you helped Michael make.

Blast that kid! you think. *Ah'm missin' out on all the fun because o' him. What's keepin' Nightcrawler, anyway?"*

Suddenly, muffled by the noise of the shaking cavern, the Sentinel's beam, and Storm's sonic pistol, you hear a cry for help from the passage overhead.

"Michael!" You fly up the vertical shaft and shine your flashlight around the passage. It's been blocked by a rock slide. Dirt is still sliding down from the roof. Michael is struggling to pull something out from under the avalanche.

"Get back!" you shout, dragging him away. Then you see what he's been tugging on—Nightcrawler's arms!

With a tremendous effort, you pull the teleporter out from under the mountain of dirt. "Kurt, ol' buddy. Are you okay?" you cry, but Nightcrawler doesn't answer.

Frantically, you roll him over to see if he's breathing. His chest rises gently, but he's unconscious. Subtract 10 from Nightcrawler's Health points.

"He got hit on the head with a rock when the earthquake started," Michael tells you as more rock falls from the ceiling.

Tucking Nightcrawler under one arm and Michael under the other, you fly back down the vertical shaft. Rock pours down the hole behind you. You consider leaving both of them on this side of the cavern, where they'll be protected by the mass field from the Sentinel and the centis on the other side, but the cavern on this side of the mass field seems to be less stable.

You have no choice but to fly outside the barrier with your passengers, where you dodge behind a boulder. Laying Kurt down and setting Michael beside him, you command the boy, "You stay right here and guard Nightcrawler!"

Storm and Wolverine are holding their own against the Sentinel and centis, but they're obviously on the defensive. Storm fires her sonic pistol to try to keep the centis away from Wolverine, but she must also protect herself

49

from the miniature monsters. Wolverine has cut deep into the Sentinel's leg as though it were a can of spaghetti, exposing wires and circuitry. In retaliation, the Sentinel has shot metal cables out from the back of its hands, wrapping them around Wolverine.

You know it won't take Wolverine long to cut himself free with his claws. "Time to turn the tables on this fight!" you say grimly. Flying straight at the Sentinel's undamaged leg, you knock the robot on its back.

As you prepare to attack the Sentinel again, the monster reaches up with its other hand and snatches you from the air! You begin pounding on its fingers, leaving great dents in them, but the Sentinel begins to squeeze you in its iron grasp. Your invulnerable body is protecting you from the pressure, but it's becoming hard to breathe.

I've ... got ... to escape his grip! you think desperately. Make a Strength FEAT roll and add the result to your Strength ability. If the total is 13 or less, turn to **73**. If it's 14 or more, turn to **92**.

44R You struggle fiercely for control of your body, but the battle is all in your head. Though you look out on the world from your own eyes, the ninja and whatever fiendish force controls his mind have complete power over you.

I must kill this man! the ninja inside you is thinking. *It is my sworn duty!*

Finally alerted to your loss of control, Wolverine leaps toward you, wrestling you to the ground. Before the ninja can react, he presses his lips against your own, setting off the automatic absorption of his powers and consciousness into your body. Instantly, you feel your own will reinforced by Wolverine's stubborn determination.

This flamin' ninja has a surprise comin' if it thinks it can take over an X-Man! you think, knowing the thought really comes from Wolverine's consciousness. *Snap out of it, girl!*

You begin to try to concentrate on how many ninjas are on the island, where they're hiding, who sent them,

and why. The scenes of death from the ninja's mind begin to fade. Whatever the thing is that controls the ninja, making his will greater than your own, begins to fall back before Wolverine's stronger will. Soon its presence disappears from your head completely, and you breathe a sigh of relief. You sit up and look around, dazed. With Wolverine's powers, you can detect a multitude of scents in the night air, including those of other Hand assassins.

Remembering the friend who probably just saved your very soul, you roll Wolverine's limp form over and try to make him more comfortable, covering him with the robe of the now vaporized ninja. Then you stand up, still clutching the ninja's sword. With Wolverine's skills at your disposal, you can now wield the weapon expertly, should you have to, to protect yourself and your unconscious companion.

In a few minutes, you sense Wolverine's powers begin to fade, and the body lying on the ground stirs slightly.

Kneeling at his side you ask, "How you feelin'?"

"Fine . . . I think. Are you all right?" he asks.

You nod. "Thanks for savin' me. I couldn't stop the thing inside me from tryin' t' kill you. I'm really sorry."

"Live and learn. I tried to tell you there was something unnatural about the Hand." He gives your shoulder a friendly squeeze and stands up.

"I found out all sorts of interestin' things," you tell him, rising to your feet. Turn to **186**.

45R Your heart is thumping hard as you watch Wolverine tear apart the mechanical volleyballs. Anxious to get in on the action, you fly toward the cluster of metal monsters with your arms outstretched, knocking hard into as many as you can. *This ought to scramble their nerves or wirin' or logic circuits or whatever they've got,* you think.

You notice that some of the spheres are firing thin blue, laserlike lights. The rays hardly register on your invulnerable body, but below, you hear Nightcrawler cry out in pain and see that he has teleported out of their path. Storm, too, seems to be trying desperately to dodge the blue bolts.

Subtract 1 from both Storm's and Nightcrawler's Health points.

From your vantage point, you can see that not all the spheres are attacking your teammates. Rapidly noting which spheres are firing the blue rays, you readjust your attack. Like a bird of prey, you drop down on the cluster of mechanical spheres.

Make an agility FEAT by rolling one die and adding the result to your Agility ability. If the total is 8 or less, turn to **139**. If it is more than 8, turn to **153**.

46S "We have an even bigger problem than the Hand," you tell Wolverine as you head toward the command center. "There may be a Sentinel about, controlling the centis."

"A Sentinel!"

"Yes. Apparently the centis were built to serve as helpers to the government-operated Sentinels."

"So that's why the little suckers looked so familiar!" Wolverine growls. "Hey! Wait a flamin' minute!" He stops dead in his tracks. "If these people are buildin' mini-Sentinels, why don't we just let them stew in the mess they've made for themselves?"

"Henry Gyrich is here," you explain. "He is responsible for security at this base. He convinced the scientists that the centis were intended as security drones and for other dangerous or mundane tasks. They did not know what his real intentions were. They are innocent dupes."

"How do we know that for sure?" Wolverine growls.

"We had a little scuffle. It ended up with Rogue absorbing Gyrich. Gyrich seems to believe there is a rogue Sentinel nearby that has taken over the centis."

You deliberately avoid relating to Wolverine all the details of your battle with Gyrich and Andrews. You have more reason to hate Gyrich than anyone here, but you are used to controlling your passions in the interest of unity. Wolverine, though, might well jump at any excuse to batter Gyrich around.

"I am not happy about leaving these people alone, even with the mass field, Logan," you continue, "but if the slightest possibility exists that there is a Sentinel here, we must search for it, and if it exists, we must kill it before it escapes this island. They are too deadly to let loose on the world."

You receive no argument from Wolverine. "Have you told the others?" he asks.

"I've talked to Dr. Laughlin about the Sentinels. He's agreed to help us."

In the command center, Michael and Dr. Laughlin are wiring together some sort of small box. Dr. Andrews is watching the outside monitors and Drs. Kirsch and Craig are programming something on the computer. Rogue stands at the foot of a table, smiling slyly at the body lying before her—Henry Gyrich.

"Doesn't he look nice?" the young mutant asks coyly. "I keep picturin' him with an apple in his mouth and potatoes all around."

"Storm?" Dr. Laughlin calls you over to where he and Michael are working. "We had an idea. For some reason the centis never stopped relaying information to our computers. I think they can be traced by their broadcast frequency. We're making you a tracking device."

"Excellent!" you reply.

"The centis should be sleeping," Michael pipes up.

"Sleeping?" you ask.

"Conserving their energy," Michael explains. "The centis use up lots of power to levitate and fire their weaponry, so they can't use very much energy at night when their solar rechargers aren't operating. Since we've never seen them at night, we assumed they must roost somewhere."

"And at night, the shadows come out," you muse. "A curious coincidence, wouldn't you say, Wolverine?"

"The centis take the day shift and the Hand work the graveyard shift," Logan says with a low whistle. "Quite a team!"

"Who are the Hand?" Dr. Laughlin asks.

"Michael's shadows," you explain. "An organization of ninja assassins."

"Wow!" Michael gasps. "Did you see them?"

"I took care of a few of 'em," Wolverine answers, "though there's plenty more out there, I'm sure."

"Gyrich is starting to wake up," Rogue informs you.

The government agent blinks, then sits up and glares at all of you. Then he turns to Rogue. "I'm adding an espionage charge to your list, woman. My head is classified information."

"Your head is a kettle o' snakes, mister," Rogue retorts.

"And it's gonna be oatmeal if you don't shut up!" Wolverine growls.

"Wolverine, Rogue! Please," you snap at them.

"Blast it!" Jesse hisses as she notices a red light starting to flash on a control panel.

"What's wrong?" Michael asks.

"The mass field's going down again," the scientist replies, rising from her chair.

"What exactly is the problem?" you inquire.

"I don't really know. The field requires a very delicate balance of energy, based on some complicated equations, so the computer controls the power feed. There must be something wrong with the program that runs things, because it keeps underfeeding power to the inner mass field, though the same program is having no trouble keeping the outer barrier up. I have to get down to the basement again to feed power manually."

"I see. You must do your best to see that it remains up while we are out hunting centis."

Jesse nods grimly, spins on her heels, and leaves the control center.

"The centis are government property," Henry Gyrich snaps. "I forbid you to destroy any of them!"

"Why don't you just come with us, Gyrich, to make sure we behave," Wolverine suggests slyly. "Then you can invite the Hand to tea—maybe invite the Sentinel, too."

"You have no proof that there even is a Sentinel," Gyrich states.

"But we know that you think there is, shugah," Rogue says sweetly. "And we aim to find the sucker and take it apart piece by piece, before you go recruitin' it or draftin' it or somethin'. That's what you hoped to do, isn't it?" Rogue taunts Gyrich with her knowledge of his mind.

"The box is finished, Storm," Michael says.

"Good. After you show me how to use it, we will prepare to leave," you reply.

If Wolverine has taken any damage, he may add 1 back to his Health points because of his Fast Healing Ability. If Nightcrawler is in the infirmary after being poisoned, turn to **28**. If Nightcrawler is exploring the base with Mrs. Taggert, turn to **137**.

Fighting to control your rage, you answer, **47N** "What you need, Gyrich, are better manners."

Then, before he can answer, you teleport yourself, Storm, and Jesse to the basement.

"Congratulations. I don't know how you managed to keep your temper," Jesse says.

"Thank you," you reply, knowing you feel better for not having hit Gyrich after all.

Turn to **75**.

48N You fire at the approaching light, wincing at the grating noise made by your sonic pistol, but the centi keeps coming. It fires a weapon of its own, a narrow, piercing blue ray that slams into your chest. Your upper body both aches and burns at the same time. Subtract 4 from your Health points.

You see Rogue zooming down the passage. She grabs the diabolical metal sphere in her hands and crushes it into a pulp of wires and mangled electrical components. "Are you okay, Kurt?" she asks you.

"I've been wounded, *Fraulein*, but it is nothing," you answer as bravely as your pain will allow.

"Lean on me, pal. Let's get back to the others before Storm gets worried and sends Wolvie to fetch us."

Turn to **87**.

49W "Please, have a seat," Dr. Laughlin offers the four of you.

As you and Nightcrawler take a chair, the elderly scientist pulls one out from the table for Storm and then one for Rogue. Both the women smile graciously as they sit down.

Privately, you think, *Hope Storm doesn't mistake his manners for harmlessness. I've got a feeling that this guy is as sharp as my claws.*

Turn to **85**.

50S Once you're safely out of the line of fire, you sneak a quick look around the control panel to see how Rogue is faring. Unfortunately, Gyrich must have had some combat training himself, for he dodges from your teammate's grasp and begins to slide across the floor. You notice that Rogue wasn't wearing her gloves. Her hands must have made contact with the agent's bare arms or face, because he stops sliding and lies still on the floor. Rogue's face becomes a study of conflicting emotions and attitudes.

Panicking, Dr. Andrews fires at Rogue with the micro-

rifle. The young woman screeches in anguish and sinks to her knees. Subtract 8 from Rogue's Health points.

You launch yourself at Andrews, intent on knocking the weapon from his grasp.

Make a Fighting FEAT by rolling one die and adding the result to your Fighting ability. If the total is 7 or less, turn to **185**. If it is 8 or more, turn to **131**.

51S
Shining your flashlight along the walls of the shaft, you discover a horizontal shaft heading south. You search for some evidence of whoever—or whatever—occupies the shaft, but the passage seems abandoned.

Sixty feet down the shaft, your way is blocked by a steel door, held shut by a large rusty padlock.

Clicking your flashlight back on your belt, you reach for your lockpicks and begin to work the pins, which must be raised before the cylinder inside will turn.

Suddenly, a high-pitched humming noise fills your ears. "Storm! We have company!" Nightcrawler whispers urgently.

"Yes. I hear it," you answer quickly, still concentrating on the lock. "A centi, I presume?"

"Just one, and moving kind of slow. I think its batteries are low."

"I hope we will not be stuck here long enough to find out," you answer.

Make an Agility FEAT by rolling one die and adding the result to your Agility ability. If the total is 8 or less, turn to **25**. If it is 9 or more, turn to **164**.

52S
You listen as your fellow X-Men tell you about the fire and the phone call. Ordinarily, you wouldn't hesitate to give the go-ahead to check out such a situation and offer what assistance you can. Breaching army security, though, is a serious matter. You've done it before, but only when it was extremely urgent. The U.S. Government and its auxiliaries don't trust mutants, and the X-Men in particular. You are widely

considered outlaw vigilantes, and your help never seems to be very welcome.

Yet if the base on Obar Island is under attack, or if there has been an accident there, people could be dying as you consider the problem.

"Well, what's the verdict, chief?" Wolverine asks. He seems eager to go, but whether he is truly concerned or not, you can't tell.

"I do not think it wise to involve ourselves, Logan," you reply. "If they say they have it under control, they obviously do not want any interference. We do not want to make more trouble for ourselves."

"But the guy was lyin'. I know it!"

"Perhaps you mistook uncertainty for untruthfulness," you suggest.

"No. He sounded very calculated, almost like a man who's been ordered to lie."

If you think you should check out the fire, turn to **98**.
If you think you'd better not get involved, turn to **166**.

53S

As Logan battles the Sentinel, you hurry to Rogue's side and kneel by her prone form. To your astonishment, she's still breathing.

"The Sentinel must have some faulty wiring for her to still be alive. Goddess be praised!" you murmur.

You look up just in time to see Wolverine being thrown away from the Sentinel's chest by an intense red beam. As your friend is propelled through the air, you rise, trying to think of some weapon you can use on the Sentinel.

The Sentinel lurches unsteadily to its feet, saying, "This unit is gravely injured, but both mutants detected have been dealt with. Retreating to secret base for repairs."

Then the creature fires the retro-rockets in its feet, skims over the hilltop, and flies off, with the surviving centis in its wake. The robots head out over the lake and disappear in the darkness.

The outer mass field must have collapsed as well as the

inner one, you realize. You also realize that the Sentinel didn't even attack you. It apparently didn't even see you as a threat. Instead, it left you behind for the Hand to deal with. If you only had your powers, you could follow it and destroy it easily.

You feel angry and powerless, but there are still things you can do. You rush down the hill to the place where you saw Wolverine land. He's alive and conscious, though he needs your help to stand up and acts very confused.

"Got to watch out for those repulsors, Jeannie!" he moans, obviously mistaking you for a former teammate, Jean Grey.

"Wolverine, I'm Storm," you correct him. "We cannot stay here."

As though to emphasize your point, a branch suddenly cracks behind you. You spin about and see a ninja, sword drawn, ready to strike!

You manage to dodge in the nick of time. The ninja whirls around quickly. You have nothing handy to defend yourself with. You grab for the crossbow Wolverine gave you earlier. The weapon is loaded, but it's tucked too tightly into your belt to draw it out quickly, forcing you to shoot from the hip. The crossbow bolt buries itself in the ninja's knee.

The assassin snarls and his knees buckle slightly, but he continues to come toward you. Before he can lunge at you, you attack him.

Make a Fighting FEAT by rolling one die and adding the result to your Fighting ability. If the total is 6 or less, turn to **7**. If it's 7 or more, turn to **63**.

54S

"Try 'X-Men,'" Gyrich orders.

Andrews looks up at him, then dutifully types what he was told. Instantly, the computer screen goes blank.

"You've crashed the computer!" Jesse cries. "It's probably trashing all the files!"

"Smart move, Gyrich," Rogue sniffs. "Ah feel so much safer knowing the security of our nation is in your hands."

"You did that somehow, to keep us from discovering the truth," Gyrich accuses Rogue.

"Right, Gyrich," Rogue replies, her voice dripping with sarcasm. "What did ah use, my telepathic computer powers?"

"Who knows what you're capable of?" the man says. "You may have stolen powers from someone besides Ms. Marvel."

Rogue flushes red with anger. You are sure she is going to hit Gyrich.

I've got to keep her from doing something foolish! you think. Turn to **160**.

55W

Your timing and angle of attack are not as perfect as you could have wished.

You succeed in smashing the ninja away from Rogue so that she does not catch the deadly powder full in the face. Unfortunately, the small amount that she does inhale is enough to start her coughing and gagging so hard that she can no longer concentrate on fighting. You must subtract 3 from her Health points.

Fortunately, you've slammed the ninja into a tree hard enough to knock him unconscious, leaving you with only two more to deal with. The fifth one moves out from behind a tree and stands next to the other. Both move in toward you, silently, efficiently.

With a *snikt*, you flash your weapons, the six adamantium claws, dagger sharp and much stronger than their steel swords.

Because the ninjas are masked, you cannot see the surprise on their faces, but they suddenly move with more caution. You parry their first set of blows easily. They are testing you now, measuring your skill as an opponent. Ordinarily, you might enjoy toying with them for a while. There's nothing you love quite as much as a fight.

But, uncertain of Rogue's condition, you decide you'd better take care of them quickly. You trap one of the ninjas' swords between two of your claws and strike out at the other attacker.

Make a Fighting FEAT by rolling one die and adding the result to your Fighting With Claws ability. If the total is 18 or less, turn to **71**. If it is 19 or more, turn to **172**.

56W

As though it were an aluminum can, Rogue crumbles the sphere in her bare hands. Some part of the sphere, however, continues to function. The steel tendrils remain tight around your wrists, and they begin to crackle with electricity. Suddenly a jolt of burning energy crawls up your arms and sets your ears ringing. Subtract 4 from your Health points.

Rogue, with her nearly invulnerable physique, grabs the tentacles and wrenches them out of their moorings somewhere deep inside the crushed sphere.

The steel bindings go limp, and the pain searing up your nerve endings subsides. The metal sphere falls to the ground.

"Oh, goll, Wolverine, I'm sorry! Are you all right?" Rogue gasps, looking at the burn marks and bruises on your wrists.

"Not your fault, kid. The thing was out to get me even if you hadn't touched it. This'll heal soon enough," you assure her, knowing that your body can recover from burns and regenerate new skin tissue with amazing speed. "If the flamin' thing had cut off my wrists, that mighta been harder to fix," you joke grimly. Though you have never tested the theory, it doesn't seem very likely that you could grow new hands.

Turn to **89**.

57R

Storm remains crouched near the ground, protecting the tracking device. Since she is the most vulnerable of all, you wonder at the courage it takes for her to face physical danger every day without any special mutant power to protect her. Turn to **202**.

58S

Mercifully, the bolt clicks open under your tender ministrations. You yank the padlock off the hasp quickly and tug at the door. The metal portal gives way with a loud creak, which echoes down the corridor. Grabbing Nightcrawler by the arm, you hurry through the doorway and slam the door behind you.

Kurt leans against the door with a sigh of relief. "You realize, of course, that if it got out there, it can probably get back in here," you tell him.

"Always the optimist," he replies. "Well, then, maybe we should get a move on."

The corridor turns east for several feet, then ends at another deep vertical shaft. Light shines up from the bottom of the shaft, and Nightcrawler teleports the two of you down easily. You find yourselves standing at the edge of a huge underground cavern.

Bright arc lights illuminate the center of the underground hall, where swarms of the strange centi-bots hover over a pit in the floor, moving in and out of the pit like busy bees.

"What are they doing?" Nightcrawler whispers.

"I can't see down into the pit from here," you reply.

"Shall I sneak up and check it out?" your partner asks.

You watch the centis for a full half a minute without answering. *Something bothers me about this situation,* you muse. *What in the world could it be?*

Make a Leadership FEAT by rolling one die and adding the result to your Leadership ability. If the total is 8 or less, turn to **182**. If it is 9 or more, turn to **176**.

59S With Rogue lying unconscious or dead and Wolverine out of action for the time being, you continue firing at the Sentinel, frantically searching your mind for something that will help you defeat the monster.

The Sentinel apparently considers its job finished. It announces, "This unit is wounded, but both mutants detected have been dealt with." Since the creature detects no mutant ability in you, it ignores you. "This unit is moving on to the mainland to continue with primary function."

The Sentinel fires the retro-rockets in its feet and flies off, with the surviving centis in its wake. Like a gigantic metal bird, it crosses over the lake and disappears in the darkness.

The outer mass wall must have collapsed, you think. Then it occurs to you with a shock that the direction the Sentinel was headed will take it right over X-Men Mansion! Even if you leave now, there's nothing you can do to warn the New Mutants in time. They'll have to face the Sentinel and its smaller helpers without your aid.

"Goddess, give them strength!" you pray. "They're going to need it." The outcome of this adventure is now out of your hands.

60N You are able to pick out four spheres that seem to lead all the others. As though they were part of a toy miniature battle, all the other spheres stay behind these leaders in tidy formations.

"Let's see if we win by capturing the flag," you suggest.

By disabling the lead robots, you hope to turn the tide of battle, but you must time your movements perfectly or risk taking damage from some weapon the robots have yet to reveal.

In a flash, you teleport yourself several feet up, just above your attackers. As you fall, you try to grab hold of each leader.

Make an Agility FEAT by rolling one die and adding the result to your Agility ability. If the result is 13 or less, turn to **24**. If it is 14 or more, turn to **67**.

61W

Soon Obar Island is nothing more than a dark shadow as your boats pull away at full speed. The trip across the water to the nearest lakeshore town, Salem Center, is a quiet one. Everyone feels subdued by the near escape from the bomb.

"You'd think we were a flamin' funeral procession or somethin'," you muse.

Gyrich has a U.S. Army bus waiting at the town's boat docks. He starts herding the research team aboard.

"Thank you all," Dr. Laughlin calls back before allowing himself to be led off by the impatient government agent.

Jesse whispers a hurried good-bye to Nightcrawler. You see her hand a small slip of paper to the blue-furred X-Man. Then she joins her associates.

You turn to Storm as the bus and its motorcade escort pull out of the small town. "Are we gonna go back and mop up the rest of the ninjas?" you ask.

"No, Logan," Storm sighs. "I think we should quit this particular game while we're still ahead."

"Whatever you say, coach," you answer, leaning back in Xavier's boat. Your adventure has come to an end.

62R

You manage to grab hold of the ninja while he is occupied with freeing his weapon from Wolverine's claws. You squeeze his arms close to his sides, forcing him to let go of his sword. It thunks to the ground, leaving Wolverine free to deliver a fast punch to the other ninja's jaw. The assassin collapses to the ground, unconscious.

Wolverine picks up a small box dropped by one of the ninjas. "Are you okay?" he asks. "This *metsubishi* is filled with poison!"

"Ah'm still a little dizzy, but ah think ah'm recoverin'. What do you want me to do with this one?" you ask, giving your prisoner a little shake.

"Hold on to him for a moment," Wolverine orders. Turn to **79**.

63S You shoot one foot out toward the ninja's head and catch his forehead with the sole of your boot. The assassin is knocked backward, but he charges back at you a moment later. Just as he lunges at you, he crumples to the ground.

Wolverine stands behind the ninja, the rock he used to clobber your enemy still in his hand. "That'll teach you to turn your back on me!" he growls.

Though he's just saved your life, you know your teammate is wounded. You have to help him back up the hill to where Rogue lies. When you reach the top of the hill, Jesse is already there with a stretcher to help bring Rogue back into the base.

"Are you okay?" she asks, looking astonished to see Wolverine still alive.

"We will live," you assure the scientist. "How is everyone inside?"

"Okay. The quake broke the connections to the mass fields, but we should be able to get them back up soon. You guys did a great job!"

"But we still lost," you say, "and the Sentinel escaped with the centis, and the Hand are still trying to kill you."

"Why don't we get inside and worry about that tomorrow?" Jesse says.

You sigh with exhaustion. You know Jesse is right. Tomorrow you will find a way to get these people off the island, and later you will find a way to track down the Sentinel and the centis and destroy them. For now, though, you are left with no choice but to hide once again in the scientists' underground fortress. For you, this is the end.

64S You watch with annoyance as Wolverine pitches wildly to Rogue.

He's going to take the safe way out and walk her, hoping to strike out Bobby, you realize.

Sure enough, Magneto, the umpire, calls four balls and sends Rogue to first base. You signal to him to call a time-out. The former would-be world conqueror, who is now filling in as mentor of the New Mutants until Charles Xavier returns from his outer space journeys, nods his assent. He holds Da Costa back from the plate until you arrive.

"Did you see what that coward did?" Roberto sniffs, scowling at the pitcher. "He did not even have the honor to let Rogue hit the ball!"

What can I say to this boy? you wonder. *How can I keep him from losing his cool when Wolverine starts to psyche him out with his macho pitching?*

Make a Leadership FEAT roll, adding the result to your Leadership ability. If the total is 10 or less, turn to **12**. Otherwise, turn to **194**.

65W Ordinarily, you would be able to dismiss your wound as minor, but you can feel a burning in your blood that indicates that your body is fighting something stronger. The blade must have been poisoned! Subtract 4 from your Health points and turn to **151**.

66N Reacting quickly, you manage to twist your body so that you can see the floor coming up to meet you by the beam of Jesse's flashlight. You land safely on your feet like a cat. Turn to **156**.

67N You grab one of the balls with your hands, a second between your feet, and wrap your tail around a third before you hit the ground, then teleport to the boat dock. Before your electronic prisoners can get their bearings and counterattack, you thrust them into the lake. Bidding them a cheery, "*Auf wiedersehen,*" you teleport yourself back to the battlefield.

Piles of scrapped robots lie near Wolverine's feet, but the remainder are packed tightly around their last leader robot so that you can't reach it without going through them.

There is a more serious problem, however. Rogue lies motionless on the ground. Storm stands over her, brandishing a charred branch to keep the robots away from your fallen comrade.

Without hesitation, you teleport to Storm's side.

"What happened?" you ask, stunned that these little monsters could harm Rogue's invulnerable body. Subtract 3 from Rogue's Health points.

Storm explains quickly, "One of the spheres touched her with a metal rod, and she collapsed in midair."

Your team leader bats away a sphere venturing too close for its own good, then adds, "She fell from about twenty feet up."

You kneel by Rogue's side to examine her. "She's still breathing," you reassure Storm. Storm nods wordlessly and continues her vigil against the spheres. *Storm is so grim and determined these days,* you think. *Is it just the responsibilities of leadership that make her so? Or is she trying to compensate for her lost powers?*

Turn to **144**.

68R Without something to brace yourself against, you doubt your super strength will be enough to hold back the weight of the earth overhead, but you struggle to keep the roof up nonetheless. Beneath you, you can see Storm has fallen, knocked unconscious by a chunk of rock. Wolverine picks her up, but he hesitates to leave you behind.

"Get out of here, Logan!" you shout. "Ah can't hold it much longer!"

Turn to **116**.

69S You feel Nightcrawler twist his body beneath your own, knowing that he is trying to protect you by absorbing the brunt of the impact himself. A split second later, he hits the ground hard. You land on top of him, badly shaken but unharmed.

"Are you all right?" you ask quickly, rolling off of Kurt and rising to your feet.

"Nothing some major back surgery won't take care of, *mein Freund*," he jokes weakly.

Subtract 1 from Nightcrawler's Health points.

You help your teammate to his feet and study him critically to make sure he isn't seriously injured.

Turn to **51**.

70R You have had contacts—unpleasant ones—with Henry Gyrich before. If Gyrich had his way, all mutants—the good along with the bad—would be rounded up and forced to live in internment camps. What makes him so dangerous, though, is the power he wields as a member of the National Security Council. He once tried to neutralize your mutant abilities, but by accident, he hit Storm instead, leaving her with only her human skills and talents. You felt guilty about Storm's loss on your behalf, but Gyrich apparently never suffered a twinge of remorse.

Dr. Craig seems completely oblivious to the scene, staring at the monitors as though no one else were about. Mrs. Taggert is nowhere in sight. Dr. Andrews is holding some sort of huge, modern rifle. Storm is seated at a table, with Gyrich standing beside her. His jacket is off, revealing a shoulder holster containing a revolver. When Dr. Andrews sees you, he swings the rifle around to point it at you.

Your teammate doesn't seem the least bit worried,

however. As a matter of fact, Storm looks somewhat amused by this petty dictator. Gyrich is obviously overheated. He has his sleeves rolled up, and sweat beads on his forehead.

"Glad to see you could join us, Rogue," the government agent says with a sneer. "By the way, you are under arrest for trespassing on government property. Maybe later we'll be able to tack on some of the older outstanding charges against you. Where is Dr. Kirsch?"

You have to laugh at his audacity. "Why should I tell you, Gyrich?"

"Dr. Kirsch is on report. She and Michael Taggert are both to be confined to their quarters so they won't make any more trouble."

"You mean so they can't let Wolverine and Nightcrawler back inside," you say. "Don't you realize that we came out here to help you, you jerk?"

"We don't need any help from mutants!" Gyrich growls. "Now, sit down. The weapon Dr. Andrews holds will damage even you. I guarantee it. Michael, your mother is waiting for you in your room."

"I'm going to go tell Jesse that you've got her microrifle!" Michael says, "Boy, are you gonna get it!"

Gyrich circles around you to move toward the door and escort Michael out of the control room, but the boy tenses defensively. Then, with a sudden burst of ferocity, he pushes Gyrich straight at you, shouting, "Here, Rogue! Catch!"

Gyrich stumbles toward you, and you instinctively reach out to grab him. It occurs to you that he might make a good shield against the weapon Dr. Andrews holds.

Make a Strength FEAT by rolling one die and adding the result to your Strength ability. If the total is 13 or less, turn to **128**. If it's 14 or more, turn to **148**.

With your free hand, you slash at the other **71W** ninja's sword, which shatters with your blow, but the ninja still grips the shard attached to the hilt. With a lightning-quick riposte, he slices deep into your forearm. What remains of his blade is stopped only by your adamantium-laced bones. The ninja loses his grasp on the hilt, and the weapon slides from your flesh to the ground. You snarl at the fiery pain shooting up your limb. Subtract 3 from your Health points, then turn to **3**.

72N You cry out in pain as you take hits from several of the blue light bolts. Automatically, you teleport to the flank of the battle, taking the nearest person, Wolverine, with you. Rogue flies into the swarm of hostile mechanoids, seemingly unbothered by the blue beams of light.

Beneath the onslaught of the blue beams, Storm doesn't seem to be faring well. She can't dodge this many attackers for long.

As Wolverine slashes at the spheres already moving toward you, you take a moment to analyze their attack. Turn to **60**.

73R Despite your efforts, you are unable to free yourself from the grasp of the Sentinel, but worse than that, you can see Michael coming out from behind the boulder, shouting for the Sentinel to let you go. Nightcrawler has regained consciousness and is trying to stop the boy, but he's too fast for the injured mutant. The Sentinel, unable to squeeze your invulnerable body to death, turns its head toward you and fires red laser lights out of its eyes. You cry out from the burning pain that racks your body. Subtract 8 from your Health points.

Suddenly, the Sentinel stops blasting you and his hand goes limp. You pull yourself out of the robot's palm. Michael comes running up to you. "Are you all right, Rogue?" he asks.

"Ah've been jellied and then fried to a crackly

crunch. No, ah am not all right, but ah'll live. What did you do to the Sentinel?" you ask, noting how still the robot is and how the centis just hover about without direction.

"I fired at its head. It disrupted the Sentinel's circuitry like it does to the centis. I got him from thirty feet away, too. Pretty good, huh?"

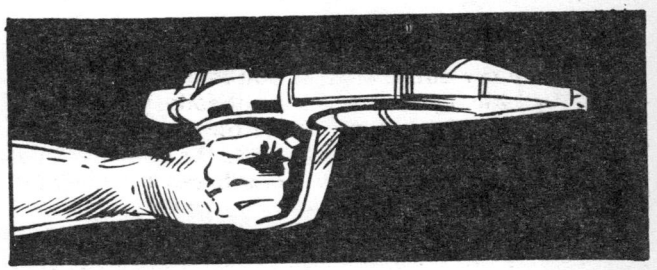

As you stare at the boy, amazed that he has no concept of how much danger he was just in, you notice Wolverine staring his way peculiarly. You wonder if it has anything to do with Michael. Turn to **201**.

"Rogue, are you all right?" you ask anxiously **74S** as you kneel beside your friend.

Rogue props her back up against the wall and looks at you, but she doesn't answer immediately. Her face is flushed bright red.

Michael hurries over with a pitcher of water and a first-aid kit. You bring the water to Rogue's lips so she can drink.

Michael pulls a plastic package out of the first-aid kit and pops something in it. "This is a cold compress. Where does it hurt most?" he asks Rogue.

Rogue points to her lower right side. Michael presses the pack against her ribs where she indicated. "The rifle works just like the blue rays the centis fire, only the centi beams are pulsed so they can't do as much damage," Michael explains. "The rifle's ray affects people as if they'd gotten a severe sunburn and been smashed at the same time in one concentrated area. One shot would kill an ordinary human being."

"Well, if there's one thing ah ain't, it's ordinary," Rogue whispers. She takes a few deep breaths and drinks some more water.

"I—I'm so sorry," Dr. Andrews says hesitantly, coming closer. You whirl about to glare at him, but Rogue tugs on your jacket.

"It's okay, Storm," she says. "I think he really means it. Gyrich had him convinced that ah was some sort of ruthless killer and we were here to destroy the base."

You still can't help feeling hostile toward the man who has injured your teammate, but you are willing to accept that he was manipulated by Gyrich. "We only came to help, Dr. Andrews!" you say in frustration.

Rogue picks herself off the floor, wincing from the pain, but her color is nearly normal and she looks as though she will live. "You may change your mind about that, boss," she says, "when you hear what Gyrich was up to here."

You look startled, wondering what Rogue could mean by that. Turn to **95**.

75N

"You said something about a mysterious underground passage," Storm says, glancing around the basement.

"Yes. It's directly beneath us."

"Beneath the basement?" Storm asks, her brow furrowed in puzzlement.

"*Ja,*" you reply.

"But according to the maps I saw earlier, it's supposed to be solid bedrock under here," Storm says.

"You must see it for yourself . . . unless you think we should wait for the others."

"No. We may not have time to wait. Right now I am concerned about how Wolverine and Rogue will get back in if we are busy elsewhere."

"Leave that to me," Jesse says. "If I can't get past Henry, or convince Gerald to countermand his order, I'll pull the plug from down here."

"But won't that leave you unprotected?"

"Just leave it to me," Jesse insists.

"Very well," Storm says, nodding. "I shall rely on you."

"I haven't had a chance to whip you up another subsonic pistol," Jesse says.

"Don't worry about it. We will be fine. If we are in any danger, we will teleport back," you reassure her.

"All right. Well," she pauses for a second, then approaches you and plants a kiss on your cheek. "For good luck," she explains, then hurries off toward the stairs leading to the upper levels.

Storm raises an eyebrow but says nothing about Jesse's peculiar behavior. "Show me this mystery place," she orders.

If you have already teleported into the passage once before, turn to **140**. If you went to get Storm before exploring below the cracked concrete floor, turn to **33**.

Mrs. Taggert brings out a first-aid kit and **76W** hands it to Dr. Laughlin. Even though she had the good sense to recognize your injuries, you can sense that she's both nervous and shy around everyone here, not just the X-Men.

"How did you get those claws?" the boy asks, staring intently at the knuckles of your glove.

"Michael!" Leona Taggert gasps. "Mind your manners."

"That's okay," you reassure her. Looking down at the boy, you explain, "I don't remember exactly. Why? Is it important?"

"I want a set for myself," Michael declares. Nightcrawler chuckles as he sorts through the first-aid kit, which Dr. Laughlin has placed on a tabletop.

"They could come in real handy, couldn't they?" Jesse muses.

"A tail would be neat, too," Michael adds.

Now it's your turn to laugh. It's impossible to tell if Kurt Wagner is blushing beneath his indigo face, but he proceeds to treat your teams' wounds in a no-nonsense way, with his tail wrapped firmly around his waist.

If you or any of your X-Men teammates took damage in the battle with the centi-bots, you may add 1 back to your Health points as Nightcrawler administers first aid. If Wolverine took any damage from the centi-bots, turn to **113**. If Wolverine's Health points are at maximum, turn to **49**.

77N You consider the wisdom of Storm's words. She stands perfectly still, looking out over the fire-ravaged, moonlit forest. She is prepared to wait patiently for however long it takes in order to do the job right. You know that's why Storm is the leader and you aren't. Turn to **197**.

78R Without something to brace yourself, you're not sure how long even your incredible super strength can hold back the mountain of earth above you. Your muscles quiver with fatigue as you shout down to the others, "Hurry! Get away!"

Wolverine yanks Storm deeper into the cavern, but the X-Men leader will not abandon you completely.

"Rogue!" she shouts back. "Get out of there—now!"

Ah'd love to oblige you, Storm, you think, *but I'm not sure ah can!*

Turn to **147**.

79R Wolverine starts to search the area, moving farther away from you until he disappears among the trees.

Whatever could he be lookin' for? you wonder. Your prisoner has gone slack in your grasp, but you aren't about to let him go.

"You're lucky we're the good guys, mister!" you growl, remembering the security guard the Hand killed. "We don't need to torture people to get information from them." Your prisoner remains silent.

You realize that all you would need to do is touch your flesh to his and absorb his consciousness for a few minutes.

There's so much we need to know, you realize. *Like who hired the Hand, and why, and how many are here, and where they're hidin'.*

But absorbing other people's consciousness can be dangerous. Sometimes another person's will takes control of your own. And, of course, you are still afraid that you may absorb someone else's being forever, the way you stole Ms. Marvel's mind and powers. *Maybe I should wait and ask Wolverine what he thinks,* you muse.

As the minutes pass, they seem to grow longer, and you begin to worry if Wolverine is all right. *Maybe he's been ambushed. There could be more Hand out there ready to jump him. This guy'd know,* you think, glaring at your prisoner. *Instead of just standin' around and waitin', maybe ah should be findin' out what this guy knows.*

If you think you'd better wait until Wolverine returns and ask his opinion about absorbing the Hand assassin's mind, turn to **167**. If you decide to do it now, turn to **10**.

80N

You teleport to Wolverine's side. He's still busy fighting the other ninja, but you don't think you can remain conscious long enough for him to finish. You grab him and teleport back to the clearing in front of the research base. As your sight begins to dim, you think, *Now I must rely on you to get me to safety,* mein Freund.

Turn to **162**.

81W

"Might as well walk Rogue," you mutter. "There's nothin' Storm can do about that." Turn to **64**.

82N Storm furrows her brow with consternation as she manipulates the wire in her hand.

You spot the centi moving toward you. "Storm!" you cry urgently. "This is not a good place to be hanging around!"

"I'm working as fast as I can, Kurt," your leader replies. "But someone apparently tried to smash this lock and damaged the mechanism."

You glance down at the battered handle of Jesse's flashlight. *Why is it that brute force always works for people like Wolverine but not for me?* you wonder ruefully. You use your body to shield Storm, holding up the piece of sheet metal in front of your chest.

Unfortunately, the centi is too smart for that. It aims a bolt of blue light at your foot. Instantly, your foot feels as though you've just stubbed all toes at once, causing you to cry out in pain. Subtract 1 from your Health points and turn to **164**.

83R "Now is our chance," Storm says, leading the two of you to the hole in the hillside. It's large enough to wriggle through. You go first, knowing you are the most invulnerable.

Soon all three of you are inside. Storm turns on a flashlight, and you discover there is room to stand.

"Must have been an old mine," Wolverine guesses, surveying the wooden beams that support the ceiling above you.

As quickly as possible, you make your way through the dark tunnel, following the signal on the centi-scan.

Suddenly, the ground begins to shake violently! Dirt rains from the ceiling, and the beams above you begin to creak alarmingly.

"The flamin' roof's crashin' in! Run!" Wolverine shouts, grabbing both Storm's and your own hand. He begins to drag you back down the passage.

With a loud rumble, the roof behind you collapses, blocking your exit. As you turn to flee out of the tunnels, a beam directly overhead cracks. Quickly, you fly up to try to hold the roof in place so your companions can escape.

Make a Strength FEAT by rolling one die and adding the result to your Strength ability. If the total is 14 or less, turn to **68**. If it is 15 or more, turn to **78**.

"Try 'X-cellent Death,' " you suggest. **84S**

Dr. Andrews looks up at you, startled. He types in the code name your teammate discovered. The computer responds by printing out a jumble of commands and a list of phone numbers and electronic instructions.

"Jackpot!" Michael shouts.

"Those first few lines have got to be the program that's been crashing the mass-field energy intake program!" Jesse exclaims.

"And those look like stock-market transactions, using funds slotted for the Obar Island research project," Dr. Craig says, pointing at the first series of phone numbers on the list.

"Congress won't like that!" Dr. Laughlin mutters.

"The next set of phone numbers are Swiss exchanges," Nightcrawler notes.

Gyrich peers at the screen. "You're right. They're deposits for Swiss bank accounts," he adds.

"Neat!" Michael exclaims.

"Are you sure, Mr. Gyrich?" you ask.

"Hey, Henry's with the National Security Council," Jesse reminds you. "He plays with Swiss bank accounts all the time, don't you, Henry?"

Gyrich doesn't answer.

"What would a Sentinel do with all that money?" you muse.

"Call Tokyo, maybe," Wolverine answers. "That's what that next phone number is."

"What's in Tokyo?" Mrs. Taggert asks.

"Ninja assassins for hire," Rogue replies pointedly.

"Storm," Wolverine whispers excitedly, "that last command on the screen—it's scheduled for midnight on the fifteenth. That's only a minute from now!"

"It looks like a transfer from a Swiss bank account to a Tokyo bank," Gyrich notes.

"Payment to the Hand for the work they're doing here, I'll bet!" Wolverine growls.

"Is there any way to cancel that transfer?" Storm asks Dr. Andrews.

Once more the scientist's fingers race over the keyboard. In moments, the transaction disappears. Everyone waits tensely until the clock indicates midnight.

Suddenly, a warning flashes across the screen. "Failure to transfer funds will result in cancellation of contract," it reads.

"Tough beans!" the Canadian super hero mutters.

" 'Project X-cellent Death Aborted,' " Dr. Andrews reads from the screen.

Rogue lets out a loud cheer. "I think we've just been saved!"

"How did you know the password?" Gyrich asks Storm suspiciously.

"Oh, Henry, for heaven's sake!" Dr. Laughlin says.

"We can't afford to take chances, Gerald," Gyrich insists. "Don't you find the similarities between the words 'X-cellent Death' and 'X-Men' suspicious?"

"Boy, am I glad I used indelible ink in the green slime!" Jesse mutters.

"I would recommend, Mr. Gyrich," you say, "that we escort these people safely off this island as quickly as possible. You can send combat troops back to mop up any remaining centis or ninjas."

"You aren't going anywhere!" Gyrich barks. "You're all under arrest for trespassing. Remember, you can't leave while the outer mass wall is still up."

"Be real, Henry," Dr. Craig says. "As long as the outer mass wall is up, we can't leave, either. I, for one, am not about to sit here cooling my heels while you rant about arresting these people."

"Me neither," Michael chirps.

All the others stare icily at Gyrich. Faced with a united front, the agent relents. "Next time I'll see to it that you don't get off so easily," he says threateningly.

"Have I really gotten off easily, Mr. Gyrich?" you ask, reminding the man that he was responsible for destroying your powers and that you haven't forgotten it.

Gyrich looks momentarily shaken but recovers quickly. "I'll meet you at the boat docks," he says to the others and leaves quickly.

Jesse lowers both mass walls, and Nightcrawler and Rogue manage to get everyone to the docks without incident. Gyrich arrives in a clean suit, carrying nothing but a briefcase.

Back in your own boat, you escort the members of the Obar Island research team across the lake to the boat docks of the nearest lakefront town, Salem Center. Gyrich has a U.S. Army bus and escort waiting for the scientists.

Before he boards the bus, Dr. Laughlin thanks all of you for your help, despite Gyrich's sour look.

"Would you do that thing with your claws one more time?" Michael asks Wolverine as he climbs the steps of the bus.

"Michael!" his mother hisses.

Wolverine chuckles. He unsheathes his claws and waves them in the boy's face. "Now, remember to mind your mother!" he orders.

"Yes, sir!" the boy replies with a gulp.

"I'm in the Palo Alto, California, phone book," Jesse whispers to Nightcrawler. "If you're ever there, look me up."

The moon has set and the stars are glittering brightly when the Army bus and its motorcade pull out of Salem Center.

"So now that that's taken care of, do we go back and wipe out any leftover ninjas?" Wolverine asks.

"Logan," you sigh, "now that Project X-cellent Death has been aborted, I have a new mission for you."

"Yeah, boss? What's that?"

"I call it 'Project X-Men Take A Break.' "

"Here, here!" Rogue seconds.

"*Ja!* Sounds like a project with much potential!" Nightcrawler adds.

"I think I can handle that," Wolverine agrees. Your adventure has ended.

85S

Dr. Laughlin seats himself across from you. "I know you took a great risk in coming here. You deserve an explanation."

"Are you under some kind of siege here?" you ask. Dr. Laughlin nods.

"We set up the facility here a month ago. We needed someplace large and secure to test the centi-bots. For a few days, everything was going just fine. The centis were judged ready to take over security, so the army unit that was stationed here left. The centi-bots started acting peculiarly almost immediately, but only a few at a time. Three days ago, they became hostile. All at once they ceased obeying our orders and began attacking us. We locked ourselves in here behind the mass field and improvised the subsonic pistols, such as Dr. Kirsch is wearing. They're crude, but they can be exceedingly effective against the centis."

From a holster at her hip, Jesse pulls out the weapon she used against the centi-bots and twirls it expertly about her finger like a Western gunfighter.

"It temporarily scrambles the centi-bots' internal control signals so they can't fly," she explains. "Those centis that are armed with particularly delicate weaponry sometimes explode."

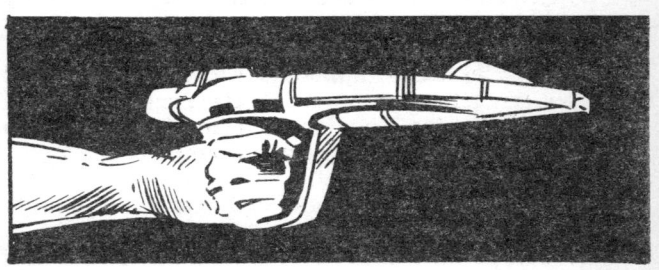

"What is this mass field you mentioned?" you ask.

"There are two, actually," Dr. Laughlin explains. "One around the building—"

"And the other around the island?" Nightcrawler guesses.

"Yes." Dr. Laughlin nods. "Both are one-way fields. You can leave this building anytime by passing right through the mass wall, but we'd have to shut down the field again before you could get back in. Nothing with a mass greater than a few micrograms can cross it."

"But why does the field around the island let people in instead of keepin' them out?" Rogue queries.

Wolverine props his feet up on the table. "A security precaution, kid," he guesses. "Am I right?"

Dr. Laughlin nods again. "The theory is that if people on the outside noticed the barrier, they would become more curious about the island."

"But if they pass through the barrier, they can't get out, and your security chief rounds 'em up for trespassin'," Wolverine guesses.

83

"Essentially, yes, though, actually, you've been the only people to defy the warning buoys," Dr. Laughlin replies.

"This field has nothing to do with keeping your mini-Frankensteins from escaping?" you ask, suspicious.

"Well, not at first," Dr. Laughlin insists. "Now, of course, it is one of the reasons we don't just lower the shields and escape to the mainland."

"What's the other reason?" Rogue asks.

"There's something else out there," Michael chimes in.

"We think," Dr. Laughlin adds.

"I saw something on the outside monitors," Michael insists.

"Shadows. It's more likely you imagined them," Dr. Andrews comments.

"If you hadn't fallen asleep on watch, you would have seen them, too," Michael replies heatedly.

Dr. Andrews turns purple with rage and starts toward Michael again. A soft whistle from Wolverine forces the scientist to reconsider his action, and he stews again in silence.

"Something else has to be out there," Jesse explains. "Two of our security personnel were missing when we locked ourselves in here, so we made up some sonic pistols so the other guards could go looking for them. They went out at night, when centi activity is lowest—the little beasts are equipped with solar rechargers, so they have to slow down after dark. We figured that, and the pistols, would make it safe enough for them. But they never came back."

Jesse points to a row of viewing screens where Dr. Craig is seated. Two monitors show the outside of the headquarters building bathed by a few stark spotlights. The rest of the screens are dark. "We haven't seen anyone but you on the security monitors," the female scientist tells you, "but we can't see much of the island at night. Whoever—or whatever—is out there must be using the cover of darkness. They must have captured our security guards."

You nod, now understanding Jesse's hurry to get indoors before the sunset.

"Unless the guards have skipped without us," Dr. Craig says sourly, still not turning around to address anyone in particular.

"Herb and Rich and Ray wouldn't do that!" Michael shouts angrily, his fists clenched as if he might hit the cynical researcher.

"Were these guards wearin' army uniforms?" Wolverine asks.

"You've seen them?" Dr. Laughlin asks excitedly.

"We found a body in the water," Wolverine answers. "Stabbed with a sword. Looked like a professional job."

Seeing the blood drain from Mrs. Taggert's pained face and the looks on the faces of the elderly scientist and the boy, you feel like kicking Wolverine. *Why must he always be so cold?* you think. Even Jesse is staring daggers at Wolverine. *She must have guessed the guards were killed,* you realize, *but she didn't want to upset the others.*

Aloud, you tell Dr. Laughlin, "I'm very sorry."

"If he was stabbed with a sword, it couldn't have been a centi that killed him," Jesse says.

"Why is that, *Fraulein?*" Nightcrawler asks.

"None of the centis has any long-bladed appendages," Jesse says. "So someone else must be out there."

Dr. Andrews bursts out, "Yes! And you just let them in, you idiot! Now they can murder us, too."

Turn to **23**.

Certain that Rogue can handle the prisoner, **86W** you scout about for some time, looking for clues as to how many more Hand agents might be around and where they are hiding.

Your sense of smell indicates that there are many more, and you can see that the forest trails have been heavily used the past day or so, but you need more precise numbers if you're going to make this island safe for the scientists back at the base.

"Better get back to Rogue. Maybe she can help me spot the ninja base from the air." When you reach the clearing, you find the prisoner lying unconscious at Rogue's feet.

"What happened?" you ask.

"He just collapsed," the young woman answers. "I think he must have swallowed a poison capsule. Then he started to dissolve."

"Yeah. They do that. Tidy for them, annoying for us," you reply while you study Rogue circumspectly. For some reason, she seems cold and distant.

Make an Intuition FEAT by rolling one die and adding the result to your Intuition ability. If the total is 19 or less, turn to **159**. If is 20 or more, turn to **195**.

87W

After a short time, you spot Rogue and Nightcrawler returning through the passage. Rogue is saying something about how the centis' blue ray weapon works—something about microwaves and boiling capillary blood.

"Who could invent so fiendish a thing?" Kurt asks.

"Jesse did," Rogue answers. "Michael says she's a weaponsmith of top caliber."

"Is it possible?" Nightcrawler asks. "She seems like such a nice lady."

"Bein' nice ain't got much to do with earning a living," you remind your friend. "Not hers nor ours, either."

Shrugging off such thoughts, Kurt turns to the issue of the centi. "How did the creature get inside the passage? Both ends were blocked."

Wolverine points to a water-filled tunnel beneath the door. "It must have come in this way when it was dry. It couldn't go back without shortin' its circuits. It was probably movin' slow because its batteries couldn't recharge down here in the dark."

Storm removes the padlock and swings the door open. The echo of its creaking hinges reverberates through the passage. On the other side of the door, there is another passageway. You cross the threshold.

Storm hands the padlock to Nightcrawler. "Lock the door behind us. Then teleport across."

"You aren't taking any chances, are you?" you ask as you listen to Kurt lock the door.

"Not when there are innocent people's lives at stake, including a child's," the X-Men leader replies.

Nightcrawler joins you in a sulfurous puff of smoke, and you continue down the next passage. It ends in another vertical shaft that leads downward. Rogue flies you and Storm down the vertical shaft, while Nightcrawler teleports beside you.

The bottom of the shaft opens into a huge natural cavern. You crouch along one edge, in a darkened corner. The other side of the vast space is well lit and swarming with centis! You draw out your sonic pistol, prepared to attack the creatures.

Storm holds you back by your sleeve. "Do you see that swarm of centis nearest us?" she asks, pointing. "They keep heading in this direction, then bouncing back. That must be where the mass field is—and it's between us and them."

"So I cross the line," you say with a shrug.

"Wait a moment. I'd like to see what they're up to first."

The centis hover over a vast pit, but you can't see inside it. Suddenly, the spherical mechanoids all begin rising up, away from the pit, as though making way for something.

"Ah have a bad feelin' about this!" Rogue mutters.

"Join the club," you whisper back.

At that moment, a huge dark form rises out of the pit. It sits up and then it stands. It is over thirty feet tall, armored from head to toe. You know, too, that it is bristling with weaponry, which it will use to destroy mutants if you don't stop it—because the thing is a Sentinel!

It's metallic voice booms through the chamber. "Inform Hand to continue Project X-cellent Death. Final payment will not be delivered until every human on Obar Island is dead. A new plan to lower mass barrier around human base is under development and will be completed before our departure."

"Who's he talking to?" Rogue asks.

Storm furrows her brow, puzzled. "It is possible that it was originally programmed to give verbal reports and cannot override its programming."

"But if he hired the Hand, how's he communicating with them? I don't see a telephone," the young woman says.

"By radio, perhaps," Nightcrawler suggests.

"It's a moot point, anyway. Why don't we just kill it now?" you suggest.

Rogue looks at you inquisitively. "You're edgy, Wolvie. Somethin' wrong?"

You're anxious to take on the Sentinel, but now that Rogue mentions it, you realize that something else is bothering you.

Make an Intuition FEAT by rolling one die and adding the result to your Intuition ability. If the total is 16, turn to **101**. If it is 17 or more, turn to **43**.

88W

You ignore the wound in your shoulder as nothing more than a flesh wound. Still, you must subtract 2 from your Health points. You catch a familiar scent in the air and realize that the ninja's blade was poisoned. Fortunately for you, your mutant healing power has healed it. Turn to **151**.

Nightcrawler pokes at the crushed metal **89W** device with a stick.

"It better stay dead if it knows what's good for it," Rogue mutters.

"There's somethin' familiar about that thing," you say, "but I can't figure out what."

"*Ja*," Kurt Wagner agrees, using the stick to flip the object over, revealing a confused mass of wires and electrical components.

"We better get going," Storm insists. "We won't be able to see much longer, and there's much to be done. Wolverine, keep a sharp ear out for any more of these things." She gives the crushed sphere a kick with the toe of her boot. "Yes. There is something familiar . . ." she murmurs.

You keep your adamantium claws unsheathed. *If I run into another one of those electronic volleyballs, I'm gonna spike it one it won't forget!* you think.

Less than a hundred yards into the forest, however, you begin to encounter an obstacle you cannot fight as easily—the fire. Underbrush crackles and sparks on both sides of the trail, and a few tree trunks are already charred and smoking at their bases. Smaller burning saplings block the path, making even walking treacherous.

"This place'd be an inferno already if it'd been summer," you note.

"*Ja*," Kurt agrees. "Lucky there was so much rain last week."

"Something very hot had to start this," Storm muses.

"Rogue, scout overhead for a clearing beyond the flames, somewhere that Nightcrawler can teleport us to."

Rogue rises above the trees and heads inland. Less than a minute later, she returns. "Two hundred yards ahead, it's just about cool enough t' walk on in our boots," she reports. "No trees t' get in your way, elf," she assures Kurt.

Nightcrawler teleports alone, to be sure of his footing on the other side, then returns to teleport first you and then Storm behind the advancing flames. Rogue flies overhead again to join the team.

All around you, the land is devastated by fire. In the twilight, it's not easy to see the footpath, now coated with ash and soot, but your sharp sense of smell picks out the scent of warm blacktop, which once kept the path clear of undergrowth. You can feel the heat of the trail even through your thick-soled boots.

The trail begins to climb up a steep hill, making it difficult to see what lies ahead, despite the fire-cleared area. Something sets the hair on your neck and arms prickling, warning you to be on your guard against danger, but you can't perceive the source of your uneasiness.

Make an Intuition FEAT by rolling one die and adding the result to your Intuition ability. If the total is 19 or less, turn to **8**. If it is 20 or more, turn to **108**.

90S The centi-bot comes at you faster than one of Wolverine's baseball pitches. Then it curves away from your makeshift bat and slams its long needle into your shoulder. A burning sensation spreads through your body, and the room begins to spin.

I've struck out! you realize. "Now it's up to Wolverine and Rogue. I hope they can find us, or at least get the people above to safety. You crash to the floor, engulfed by darkness and deep sleep. . . .

91R You return to the command center, cradling Nightcrawler gently in your arms. You realize that Storm needs him here to keep an eye on things for the X-Men. You hope he'll be strong enough to keep Gyrich from bullying the researchers into doing something that will interfere with the X-Men's plans.

Jesse has returned from the basement. She and Mrs. Taggert fuss over Kurt, making sure he is comfortable on the couch they've made up for him. Nightcrawler, of course, is eating up the attention.

It's past midnight when you emerge back out into the open air. The moon is under a heavy cloud cover. Outside the range of the base's spotlights, all is pitch-black.

"No sign of the wall-bashing ninja," you joke.

Wolverine sniffs the air. "He's out there, all right. And he's brought along some of his friends."

Storm fiddles with some dials on the tracking device. "I'm not getting any signals on the centi-scan up here. We'll have to go down the hill."

You begin picking your way through the burned forest. Suddenly, you hear a whistling noise off to your left. Wolverine knocks Storm to the ground and flattens himself over her, but it isn't much cover against the rain of silver darts headed right toward them.

Ah have to shield them! you realize, and you leap into the path of the missiles aimed at your friends. Make an Agility FEAT by rolling one die and adding the result to your Agility ability. If the total is 7 or less, turn to **193**. If it is 8 or more, turn to **135**.

Calling on all your strength, you bend back the **92R** Sentinel's index finger. The metal creaks, then snaps loudly. You slip out of the creature's grip and fly to a safe distance.

You see Michael pop up from behind the boulder where you hid him. He fires at some centis over your shoulder, and they explode in midair. Nightcrawler has regained consciousness, and the blue mutant pulls the young boy back down before he is hit by attacking centis.

Assured of the child's safety, you go about your work. You land beside Wolverine, who is grinning fiendishly as he destroys what's left of the Sentinel. You wonder, *Is Wolvie enjoyin' this as much as I am, or is he thinkin' about somethin' else?* Turn to **142**.

93N You teleport away from the Sentinel, taking with you only the robot's head. You reappear just outside the pit, only a few yards away. The strain of carrying so great a weight, however, is too much for you. Completely exhausted, you watch as a fountain of sparks shoots up from the pit and frenzied centis spin about in confusion.

Unfortunately, some of the monstrous spheres realize you are the cause of their trouble, and they begin attacking you with blue rays, gas, blinding light, electrical shocks, darts, and a myriad of other diabolical devices. Too weak to teleport away, let alone fight them off, you begin to lose consciousness.

Storm and the others will have to handle it from here, you think just before you black out and your adventure comes to an end.

94S You and your fellow X-Men follow the woman, Jesse, through a tangled mass of warm, stuffy corridors, up and down staircases and elevators, and in and out of empty waiting rooms. Beside you, Wolverine frowns. You wonder if he feels as lost as you do. Turn to **41**.

95R "Well, enlighten me, child," Storm orders you.

"These people were here buildin' these centis because Gyrich told them that the centis would be used just for security purposes—hostage situations, stuff like that."

"That's right," Michael says.

"Well, Gyrich had other plans for these critters," you explain.

"Such as?" Storm asks, all attention.

"How about a riddle? What else, besides centis, is steel-gray and purple, made of metal, and likes to attack mutants whenever it gets a chance? Need a hint? Think *real* big."

"Goddess!" Storm whispers. "Not a Sentinel!"

"Yep!" you say, nodding. "Gyrich picked out the name centi 'cause the little monsters were supposed to be one one-hundredth the size of a Sentinel. They're programmed to take orders from Sentinels. That way, the Sentinels could send them into tiny spaces—elevators, taxis, sewers, gift boxes from Bloomingdales. . . ."

"Are they obeying a Sentinel now?" Storm asks.

"Gyrich isn't sure. As far as he could establish, there aren't supposed to be any government Sentinels near enough to send commands along the frequency the centis receive."

"But it is quite possible there is one about—left over from an old battle," Storm guesses.

"And if it's damaged, the centis can repair it," you warn her.

"Now I am getting concerned for Wolverine's and Nightcrawler's safety," Storm says.

"Me, too," you whisper.

"The Sentinels were built to capture or kill any mutants they find," Storm muses. "The X-Men have defeated the deadly giant robots in the past, but only when they worked as a team. If there's a Sentinel out there that Gyrich doesn't know about, it might be controlled by some super villain, but more likely it's a rogue, deciding its actions for itself. And with Sentinel logic, devoid of compassion or pity, the creature can be a ruthless killer of mutants—or anyone else who gets in its way."

"The one who's in the most trouble now is Gyrich," Jesse's voice says. She's standing in the command center doorway, listening to your conversation. "When he comes to, I'm going to kill him."

"You'll have to take a number," you joke grimly.

"I told him I wouldn't work on any Sentinel projects,"

the female scientist goes on. She scoops up the microrifle and turns to Dr. Andrews. "Don't touch my toys again, Jonathan," she warns, waving the rifle under his nose.

Jonathan backs away, but then he says, "If there is a Sentinel controlling the centis, why did they try to destroy us? We're not mutants."

"That's true," Jesse agrees. "Why, there are even those among us who are throw-backs to the Neanderthals!" She casts a glowering look at Gyrich.

"The Sentinel could be trying to insure that no one discovers it," Storm explains. "Eventually, it will have to get inside the base to destroy the outer mass wall in order to escape. Our job will be to find it and destroy it. But first we must wait for Wolverine and Nightcrawler. I wonder what they are doing now. . . ."

Turn to **158**.

96S Something explodes behind the Sentinel's face. Pieces of its head shake loose, and sparks fly out from the holes created. The Sentinel drops Rogue to the ground, then topples over slowly. It lies completely still but for the sound of the shorting electrical wires in its mechanical brain.

The centis hover in midair, as though stunned, then they all land on the ground, humming softly, apparently no longer hostile.

"Nice shootin'!" Wolverine shouts, whistling in admiration.

You shrug. "There was nothing else I could do."

"These little critters look like they're bowin' down to you as their new master," he teases.

"Please, Logan. The thought is too disgusting. . . . Rogue! Is she alive?" The two of you hurry to the girl's side. Storm kneels beside the girl's body. Turn to **121**.

97S You smash your makeshift bat across the speeding centi-bot, sending it crashing against the wall. It falls to the ground in pieces. You kick at the remains with one foot, your bat still at the ready, prepared to bash it again should it so much as make a sound.

"Be careful, Storm," Nightcrawler cautions.

"Do not worry, Kurt. I believe I've knocked this one out of the stadium." You dig through the innards of the centi-bot until you discover a likely-looking piece of metal. Grinning, you return to Nightcrawler's side and slip the key into the lock of his manacles. It turns easily, and you pull the bindings off your companion's limbs.

"*Danke schoen!*" Nightcrawler says as he rises shakily to his feet. You wonder if he'll be able to continue. Turn to **110**.

98S You cannot stand by while innocent people are in danger, even if it means more trouble for the X-Men. Besides, you can sense the team members in front of you champing at the bit. Rogue, especially, can hardly contain her excitement. She looks to you as if she might fly away the moment you give the go-ahead.

"Very well," you agree. "We'll check it out." Turn to **19**.

99R You bite back your frustration. You know Storm is right. The helicarrier incident ultimately led to Storm being robbed of her powers by an overly enthusiastic government agent.

Wolverine says nothing, but he doesn't look pleased. He fails to join the rest of you for the barbeque in the back yard that night.

The next morning, Storm corners you and Nightcrawler. "When was the last time you saw Wolverine?" she demands.

You have to think for a moment. Yesterday is already a blur in your mind. "When we were discussin' the fire on Obar Island," you answer finally. "Why?"

"I cannot find him, and his bed hasn't been slept in," Storm explains.

"You think he went out there alone?" Nightcrawler asks.

"He is gone. So is the sailboat," Storm says simply.

The three of you jump in the motorboat and set out for Obar Island. When you get there, you find that the fire has done extensive damage to the forest and apparently destroyed the base entirely. The burned-out husks of three army barracks stand on a hilltop, while a fourth building seems to have caved in from below and then burned. You volunteer to make a quick exploration of the island.

"It must have had several underground levels," Nightcrawler says. "I detect the smell of many chemicals in the air. Perhaps there was a laboratory explosion before the building collapsed and burned."

Storm shakes her head sadly. "No one could have lived through that inferno," she says, then notices you returning. "What did you find, Rogue?" she asks.

From the air, you noticed something strange. "Ah saw some clothes scattered about in the woods. They looked like red uniforms of some sort, but with no one in them. Ah spotted about ten of them from the air, but not one person. There was no trace of Wolvie."

The three of you spend the rest of the day on the island rummaging about, but nothing more comes to light. By late afternoon, Storm calls a halt to the search before the authorities show up and blame you for the damage.

You return to X-Men Mansion, but the story of Obar Island and the fate of your companion Wolverine remains a mystery. Your adventure is over.

"The basement is mostly used for storage," **100N** Jesse explains. "Of course, there's the air-conditioning unit, the generator, and the mass fields equipment as well."

Jesse flips on the stairway light, and you follow her into the bowels of the complex. This is the only level that does not remind you of a maze. One giant room, the size of a football field, contains a few piles of odds and ends plus the three major pieces of equipment Jesse told you about.

You pause at the power generator. It's like none you have ever seen before. Shaped like a dodecahedron about four feet across, it appears to be a dark shadow. Only the power lines snaking out from the sides reveal its function. "What fuels it?" you ask.

"Dilithium crystals," Jesse answers.

"You're joking!" you reply, knowing such a power source is fictional.

"You're right, I am, but I'm not allowed to tell you the real fuel. It's strictly top-secret and experimental. And this is the mass-field generator for the building," Jesse says, pointing to one of two metal pieces of equipment. "Creating the field requires a delicate balance of power, which is controlled by computer, but every now and then some bug in the program turns up, and the computer stops feeding power to the field. Then I have to come down here and adjust the power intake manually. It's annoying. The computer program should work perfectly. I wrote it myself."

You peer around the dark room thoughtfully. The floor is made of concrete, and you spot a large crack a few feet over. You glance at Jesse questioningly.

"It's just a thaw-and-freeze crack," Jesse says, shrugging.

"This far underground? Put your hand over it," you direct her.

"There's air coming up! Warm air!" she exclaims.

"*Ja*. See how the crack forms a complete circle? This could be a door." With a long piece of wire, you discover that there is a large space beginning a foot beneath your feet, but try as you might, you can't pry up the huge cement block, not even with a crowbar Jesse digs out of a tool box. You can't help but wish Colossus were here.

"Shall we try a sledge hammer?" the scientist asks.

"No. For now, it's probably best to keep it covered. I can teleport down there easily enough."

"You aren't going down there without me?" Jesse asks indignantly.

"*Ja, Fraulein*. That is my job. Yours is up here."

"But shouldn't you tell Storm first?"

"I'm just going to do a quick reconnaissance. Be back in a second."

Jesse stomps her foot angrily on the cement. "I don't think that's wise," she insists. "It might be dangerous." She looks and sounds so much like Storm that you reconsider your actions.

If you want to take a quick look below without a partner, turn to **136**. If you think you'd better let Storm know what you've found first, turn to **29**.

101R

"I can't tell," Wolverine whispers to you. "Maybe it's just the buzzing noises those little monsters make."

Now ah'm gettin' edgy, you think, worried that there is something wrong that Wolvie can't pinpoint.

But you don't have any more time to think about Wolvie, because the next moment, the Sentinel raises its hands to the ceiling, and a searing red ray shoots out of its palms. The cavern shakes all about you, and chunks of the walls and ceiling begin to shower down on you. Over the Sentinel's head, another vertical shaft begins to form.

"We must stop him!" Storm orders. "The mass field cannot protect the base from an earthquake!"

"No argument here," Wolverine says, grinning. He tenses his muscles, then dashes toward the Sentinel with his claws unsheathed. At the same instant, Nightcrawler teleports atop the monster's shoulder, while you fly straight at its chest.

You can hear the grating noise of a sonic pistol just before you smash into the Sentinel. The Sentinel proves to have extremely heavy armor that even you cannot penetrate, and you merely bounce off. The creature, though, caught unawares, falls backward into the pit, shouting, "Warning! Contact with mutants! Primary objective: Destroy all mutants!"

Immediately, the centis swarm all about you, firing their blue rays at you, apparently protecting their leader.

How much longer, you wonder, *before they realize I'm immune to these things and use something else against me?*

Fortunately, you never learn the answer to that question. The grating noise of a sonic pistol sounds once more, and centis all about you explode in midair.

Nice shootin', Storm! you think. *Now I can concentrate on the Sentinel!* You look down to salute your team leader, only to discover it was not she who fired at the centis. "Michael!" you scream.

There below you stands Michael Taggert, firing a sonic pistol at every centi he sees. What he doesn't see is the prone Sentinel's hand stretching toward him!

You have only scant seconds to save the boy from the robot's clutches. You swoop down.

Make an Agility FEAT by rolling one die and adding the result to your Agility ability. If the total is 6 or less, turn to **165**. If it's 7 or more, turn to **111**.

102R

You offer to help fly people to the boat docks. Michael is thrilled, but Storm feels that teleportation would be safer. Nightcrawler uses up most of his energy teleporting everyone from the base to the boat docks.

Your boats are just pulling away from Obar Island when Wolverine's head jerks up suddenly. "Ninjas!" he whispers tersely. "Three of them, in those bushes next to the beach!" Suddenly he shouts, "Heads up, Rogue! Missile coming your way!"

You see missile arcing toward you, glistening in the

moonlight. About the size of a softball, it looks like a miniature centi-bot. You're not sure just what it is, but you suspect it would be better if it landed in your own invulnerable hands than in one of the boats filled with people.

You must make an Agility FEAT by rolling one die and adding the result to your Agility ability. If the total is 7 or less, turn to **169**. If it is 8 or more, turn to **9**.

Apparently the poison acts faster than your **103W** body can cope with it. You must subtract 2 more from you Health points. The pain continues to increase slightly, but finally it levels off. However, the bindings around your wrists continue to tighten.

Fortunately, Rogue quickly recovers from her momentary blindness. She blinks a few times before she can focus, but then she reaches out once again to grab the sphere. Turn to **56**.

"I'm sorry, Storm, but I don't think we can **104N** afford to delay. Don't wait up for me," you say, then teleport back inside the cavern, back to the pit in which the Sentinel lies. You stand just above its head.

It looks a lot bigger close up, you think.

This particular Sentinel apparently relies on visual contact to alert himself to mutants, because it fails to notice your presence. It is now issuing verbal com-

mands. "Continue with Operation Code Name X-cellent Death," the robot intones as you sneak closer to it.

The Sentinel's orders are interrupted when a centi seems to spot you and twitters excitedly. The Sentinel tries to crane its massive neck about to see what has excited the centi.

"This is it!" you mutter and leap onto the Sentinel's head, throwing your arms about its face. You have never teleported something this massive before, but you are committed to it now.

You must make a Teleportation FEAT by rolling one die and adding the result to your Teleportation ability. If the total is 11 or less, turn to **93**. If it's 12 or more, turn to **123**.

105N
You teleport to Wolverine's side and collapse immediately at his feet.

"Kurt!" he gasps. He quickly dispatches the ninja he is fighting with a savage slash. Then he kneels by your side.

"I . . . do not feel very well," you gasp.

"Hang in there, pal! I'll get you back to the base," Wolverine says, but his voice sounds a long way off. You know he'll do everything in his power to save you, but as you fade into a deep slumber, you pray that he won't end up risking his life for your own. Your adventure has ended.

106W
Your claws slice into the metal armor of the Sentinel's leg, but not deeply enough. The robot remains standing. However, it does drop Rogue to the ground.

Great! you think. But then the monster turns its attention toward you. The next thing you know, you are flying through the air, kicked far across the burned hillside by the Sentinel's giant foot.

You fall to the ground with a sickening thud. You realize that your body will heal the damage you took from the fall. *But what can Storm do to defend herself against that thing?* you wonder as you fade into unconsciousness. Turn to **59**.

107R

You reach out for the ninja, but he slips beneath your arms and dives into the dark undergrowth. "Either that powder is making me clumsy, or this guy is really fast," you mutter. You dive in after him, but he seems to have vanished in the brush.

In the meantime, Wolverine has dispatched the fifth ninja with a few well-timed punches. The red-robed figure crumples to the ground.

"One got away," you say apologetically.

"It doesn't matter. Are you all right? The powder you breathed from the *metsubishi* was poisonous," Wolverine explains, pointing to the small box that the ninja dropped.

"Ah think ah'm okay. Just a little dizzy, but it's fadin'. Your arm all right?" you ask, seeing the blood already clotting on the surface of Wolverine's wound.

"It'll heal," he assures you. Turn to **117**.

108W

At the very limit of your range of hearing, you sense a vibration that is causing the sensation of danger you feel. You realize with a start that it is the same humming noise made by the electronic sphere that attacked you earlier, but now it is increased twenty-fold!

"Incoming volleyballs! A whole horde of them!" you shout to the others. You reach the top of the hill in two leaps, charging the onslaught of miniature robots as they swoop down upon you. Your adamantium claws gleam in the rays of the setting sun as you slash upward in a berserk fury.

Make a Fighting FEAT by rolling one die and adding the result to your Fighting With Claws ability. If the total is 18 or less, turn to **124**. If it is 19, 20 or 21, turn to **134**. If it is 22 or more, turn to **27**.

109R *Ah'd better deal with this one,* you think, turning your body so that it shields everyone from the ball. Already you can feel the ball heating up. *There's no time to throw it!* you think.

You squeeze the tiny sphere with all your might. Make a Strength FEAT by rolling one die and adding the result to your Strength ability. If the total is 13 or less, turn to **13**. If it is 14 or more, turn to **112**.

110N As soon as you have your arms about Storm, you teleport the two of you back outside, to the bluff at the edge of the base clearing. The moonlight shines about you, and the night is still.

"I have a bad feeling about this, Kurt," Ororo says slowly. "What was in the pit?"

"Surely you have guessed already," you reply. "It was a Sentinel."

Storm nods her head. Sentinels—giant robots constructed to capture or destroy all mutants—have plagued the X-Men for years. Their masters have included madmen, villains, and even on occasion the U.S. Government. But even worse, sometimes the Sentinels control themselves. When this happens, they are merciless and without regard for any who get in their way, human or mutant.

"It looks as if it was damaged badly in some battle," you explain. "Perhaps it's even one we've fought before. All the centis were busy rewiring it and welding it back together. It was just lying there, looking up at me. I guess I panicked for a moment. I wasn't expecting it."

"I should have realized," Storm chides herself.

"How could you know?" you ask.

"The centi-bots," Storm says. "Remember, when we first saw them, they seemed familiar somehow. They are like miniature Sentinels. They have a variety of weaponry, they can fly, and they attack mutants. Some of them are even painted in the same colors. They are little helpers for the Sentinels."

You shake your head in confusion. "I cannot believe it. How could Jesse build such monsters?"

Storm squeezes your shoulder gently. "She may merely be an innocent dupe. Gyrich could have lied to the scientists here, misleading them into believing the centis were supposed to be guards."

"But why did the centis start attacking the base?" you wonder.

"It is possible they fell under the command of the Sentinel below, and the giant robot does not obey Gyrich," Storm suggests.

"We have to deal with the Sentinel," you declare.

"We will. When Wolverine and Rogue get back."

"There may not be time," you reply. "The Sentinel looked as though it was almost completed, and if the mass wall collapses, the monster will make short work of the people in the base. We must destroy it first!"

"Nightcrawler, we must wait. We have defeated Sentinels in the past, but that is only because we fought as a team. It is too dangerous to try alone."

You know you could destroy the Sentinel now if you could just get to it while it is still comparatively inactive. You could execute it before it had a chance to harm any of your friends. It wouldn't be easy, but you wonder if you dare wait for Wolverine and Rogue, no matter what your leader says.

If you want to try to destroy the Sentinel now, turn to **104**. If you think you'd better wait as Storm suggests, turn to **77**.

111R You scoop Michael out of the path of the Sentinel's groping hand and land in a far corner of the room, away from the battle.

Nightcrawler teleports to your side. "I'll take charge of the boy," he says quickly. "You take care of the Sentinel!"

"Thanks, elf," you reply. You put Michael down and fly back into the battle, glancing back to see Nightcrawler clamping his hand on the boy's shoulder to make him stay put. Turn to **126**.

112R

The sphere feels as though it were solid metal, but finally it crushes in your hands as though it were a raw egg. A slimey gel gushes out over your gloves and the front of your costume. Metal wires inside the crushed missile spark uncontrollably, igniting the gel that covers you. In moments, your whole body is ablaze. You realize that the fire won't harm your invulnerable body, but it will destroy your clothing.

"Excuse me, y'all. Suddenly ah feel like takin' a quick moonlight swim."

You plunge beneath the cool waters of the lake. When you come to the surface, you notice that the water has washed the chemical from your body, but patches of the gel float on the surface, still burning eerily in the dark.

Nightcrawler offers you a hand and starts to help you back into the boat. "It's a little early for a swim, isn't it, *Fraulein?*" he teases. "How's the water?"

"Why don't you find out for yourself?" you reply, giving him a playful tug toward you.

"*Nein,* thank you," he laughs, pulling you into the boat.

Wolverine drapes a towel around your shoulders as the *Lilandra* pulls away from the island. "Nice catch, kid," the Canadian says as he tousles your wet hair playfully. Turn to **61**.

113W

Kurt uses some sort of spray on the bruised areas of your flesh. The pain is relieved immediately, though the damage beneath will take a little more time to heal.

Determined to take advantage of your momentary safety, you sit down on a chair and stretch out to relax, conserving your energy so your body can heal more quickly.

Make a Fast Healing FEAT by rolling one die and adding the result to your Fast Healing ability. If the total is 21, turn to **15**. If it is 22, 23, 24, or 25, turn to **183**. If it is 26 or more, turn to **30**.

114N

You feel your temper boil dangerously. *I've had it!* you decide. *Gyrich has asked for this!*

You crack your fist across Henry Gyrich's jaw, and the security council member reels across the room. Before he can rise to his feet, you teleport to the basement with Jesse and Storm.

"I wish you hadn't done that," Storm says.

"I am sorry to disappoint you, *mon capitaine*, but it felt so good!"

"It felt good for me, too," Jesse says with a grin.

Storm shakes her head without further comment. You know she is right, though. Even if Gyrich had it coming, violence never solves such a problem; it can only make it worse. You must subtract 1 from your Karma Pool. Turn to **75**.

115W

Your fist connects with the ninja's mask, and he stumbles back and collapses against a tree. His companion lunges at you with a sword. Giving the mental command that unsheathes your claws, you manage at the last instant to parry his attack on the adamantium daggers of your left hand. Then you hack at his blade arm with the claws on your right hand. The ninja makes a guttural noise you hope is an expression of pain.

Turn to **151**.

116W

You hesitate a moment too long, and the hill Rogue has been holding back comes crashing down on top of you.

It takes several long seconds for the dirt and rock to settle about you. You are hurt, but at least you're not buried by the avalanche. A tiny pocket of air-filled space surrounds you. In the dark, you feel Storm's hand in your own. "You all right, darlin'?"

"I am breathing," Storm whispers. "Rogue?" But Rogue doesn't answer. You hear Storm scrabbling around until her hand falls on her flashlight. She turns it back on and slides the beam around the area. "Logan, there's Rogue's hand, sticking out from that pile of dirt!"

You scrabble furiously with your claws until you uncover Rogue's head.

Storm brushes the dirt away from her face. "She's still breathing!" the X-Men leader says with a sigh of relief.

"With half a mountain on top of her, yet. That's what I'd call invulnerable!" you reply grimly. You dig dirt away from the young woman's torso until you are stopped by some large rocks piled up against Rogue's lower back. "I don't dare try to slash through these, 'Roro. I could catch her by accident or bring down the roof the rest of the way. We'll need some equipment to get her out," you explain. "At least I feel some air comin' in here from deeper in the cave. We can probably dig our way out that way."

"I wonder if the centis or a Sentinel caused the quake," Storm whispers.

"If that's the case, Nightcrawler's goin' to find out

soon enough," you reply.

"Yes," Storm answers. You can see how worried she looks. "We will have to start digging," she says.

"It could take all night," you warn. "Maybe even longer."

"But it's all we can do," Storm points out. "The sooner we get started, the better."

The two of you begin digging through the dirt. As you dig, you can't help but wonder how Nightcrawler and the others at the base are faring. *I hope it's better than we are,* you think, but you fear that your adventure has come to an unfortunate end.

Wolverine bends over the body of the first **117R** ninja and pulls off his robe. The cloth comes away easily. With a start, you realize that there's no one in it anymore!

"What—what happened to him? Wasn't he real?"

"The Hand have got this tidy way of removin' the evidence and keepin' prisoners from being taken. Their bodies dissolve if they die or even go unconscious. Could be some sort of virus or somethin'."

"This is no fun anymore," you declare, staring at the bodies of the other Hand agents on the ground. Before your eyes, a mist rises from their robes and the cloth begins to collapse.

"How horrible! Do they know that's going to happen to them?" you gasp.

"Probably. These are really fanatic people we're dealin' with. Here, put this on."

Wolverine hands you the ninja's robe. You almost shrink from its touch. *Don't be silly, girl,* you chide yourself. *Can't go flyin' around with my costume in tatters. Ah definitely do not want to brush against any of these sickos now and absorb their minds by accident.*

You put on the robe, surprised to find that it is quite comfortable. "What now, boss?" you ask.

"I want to scout out the place from the air," Wolverine tells you.

109

You nod, pick your partner up in your arms, and take off. Soaring above the trees, you consider that another man in his position might feel awkward being carried around by a female super hero, but Wolverine accepts your powers matter-of-factly. He's possibly one of the most self-sufficient people you have ever met. Still, he realizes how important good teamwork can be. *Teamwork may be the most important thing goin' for us right now. I wonder how the others are doin'?* you think. You take one last glance at the empty robes lying on the ground before you fly off above the trees, heading back to Storm and Nightcrawler. Turn to **14**.

118S

It would be dishonest to say you weren't amused at the spectacle of Gyrich fallen prey to so silly a prank.

Jesse's had her fun, but now, I fear, she must face the consequences.

Dripping the gooey green substance across the floor, Gyrich moves to the control panel where Jesse is sitting and pushes a button. Immediately the lights stop flashing and the Klaxons cease blaring.

"You did this!" the government agent accuses the female scientist vehemently.

"Me?" Jesse asks, feigning shock.

"I'll get even with you, Kirsch!" Gyrich shouts.

You interrupt Gyrich's ranting. "Not to change the subject, but we discovered something unusual about the centi-bots—something I suspect you knew Mr. Gyrich, but perhaps you didn't inform Dr. Kirsch of."

Gyrich freezes and says nothing.

"The centi-bots no longer obeyed your commands," you explain calmly to the scientists, "because they had a new master—an injured Sentinel hiding below this base. We found the centis repairing it."

Dr. Kirsch rises from her chair and stands face to face with Gyrich. Her fists are clenched, and her voice is low and angry. "So that's why they had such an unusual command frequency! I told you I wouldn't work on any

Sentinel projects! You told me the centis were for guard duty and hostage situations only. You lied to me!"

Jesse raises her fist, but Kurt wraps his arms about her shoulders. "*Nein, Fraulein,*" he whispers. "You don't want to soil your hands on the likes of him."

Jesse takes a deep breath. "You're right," she says more calmly.

"I assure you, I knew nothing about any Sentinel beneath this base," Gyrich says.

"You know about lots of other Sentinels, though, don't you, Gyrich?" Wolverine growls.

"Naturally," the government agent answers coolly.

"Well, what about this Sentinel?" Mrs. Taggert asks. "Will it attack us?"

"No," you assure the woman. "We destroyed it. That should take care of the danger from the centis as well. Many of them acted confused by their robot master's demise. The centis may even obey you again."

"Then we can turn off the outer mass field and leave the island," Dr. Laughlin says.

"There's still the Hand," Rogue warns.

"With the mass fields down, I can teleport everyone to the boats and we can escape the island easily," Nightcrawler offers.

"They may be watching the boats," Dr. Andrews argues.

"I never met a ninja I couldn't handle," Wolverine interjects. "Besides, the cover of darkness will work just as well for us as it does for them."

"We can't surrender this base to the Hand," Gyrich declares.

Dr. Laughlin looks pleadingly toward you. It's obvious he's anxious to leave the besieged base and get his people to safety, but he needs you to overrule Gyrich.

Getting around the government agent will not be easy. He distrusts you even more than he fears the Hand.

Make a Leadership FEAT by rolling one die and adding the result to your Leadership ability. If the total is 10 or less, turn to **31**. If it's 11 or more, turn to **181**.

119W *That girl is just itching to clobber the ball,* you realize, noting how Rogue clenches the bat. A gentle spring breeze wafts the scent of her excitement to your nose. Even more interesting, though, is the admiration you see in Roberto Da Costa's eyes as the young man watches the batter preceding him.

If I walk Rogue, you think, *Roberto is goin' to be offended, an' think he needs to defend her honor. He may actually psyche himself up an' bat better. Then I'll hafta go up against Petey.* Peter Rasputin, also known as Colossus, though Russian-born, has adapted to the American game with a vengeance. He's an awesome batter. And walking Petey would tie the game. After Petey would come Sam Guthrie of the New Mutants, a pretty level-headed kid with a good eye. *I'm goin' to have to try something tricky here,* you say to yourself

You pitch the first two balls way outside. Rogue squints her bright, green eyes and stares daggers at you, certain that you intend to walk her. Then you throw one of your curves, which she misses by a fraction of an inch. Possessing the seventh sense that once belonged to Ms. Marvel before Rogue stole it from her, the girl can sometimes anticipate things before they happen.

"Anticipate this if you can, kid," you whisper and throw an easy pitch with absolutely nothing on it.

Rogue swings with the fury of the righteous, plus the super strength she also stole from Ms. Marvel. Part of the ball flies off toward the right infield, but the other half, the jacket, flops to the ground, near home plate.

Rogue takes off for first, then slows as she rounds the bag, uncertain if it's safe to continue. She decides to stay put.

Play halts as Magneto steps onto the field. Once the leader of the Brotherhood of Evil Mutants, the hopefully reformed Master of Magnetism is now filling in for the space-faring Charles Xavier as mentor of the New Mutants. Xavier has provided him with a cover identity, as his nonexistent brother, Michael Xavier. Magneto plucks the ball's shredded cover from the ground and

walks toward the pitcher's mound, beckoning with his umpire's cap for Storm and Rogue to approach.

"I believe this is what is known as a rule-book double," Magneto says, raising an eyebrow in your direction.

Magneto reminds you of Professor X. Both of them are tall, blue-eyed, and eggheads. Still, you shift just a little nervously under the older man's gaze. He's pretty shrewd.

"Good call, Magneto!" Rogue dances over to second base. Storm walks more thoughtfully to third.

"We shall have to be more careful in the future as to the quality of the balls we pitch to Rogue," Magneto warns you.

"Sure, Mikey," you answer with a grin. Magneto scowls at the nickname and walks back behind home plate.

Roberto Da Costa walks cockily up to the plate, certain that he can bat as well as, if not better than, Rogue. Your original estimate of the solar-powered mutant soon proves correct. You throw two straight pitches close to his body. His temper flaring, he loses his concentration. A few fast balls and a curve later, and he's out.

"Pretty sneaky pitching, Logan," Storm congratulates you.

"Thanks, Ororo. I try to keep my hand in."

"If you'll excuse me, I think I have some wounded egos to salve," the X-Men leader says.

You watch your defeated opponent stride off as your teammates approach to congratulate you. "Nice pitchin', Wolvie," Kitty Pryde chuckles, punching you fondly in the arm.

Just as Nightcrawler reaches out to congratulate you, you catch a smell in the air that can only mean trouble. Turn to **150**.

120S You can't seem to open the lock. Behind you, Nightcrawler fidgets nervously. Turn to **82**.

Rogue is deathly pale and still. "How is **121W**
she?" you ask.

"She's breathing," Storm replies softly, "but just barely."

You hear the swish of an automatic door. Turning, you see Jesse leaving the headquarters building carrying a stretcher.

"It's not safe out here!" Storm warns her. "The Hand are still nearby."

"Then we'd better get inside with Rogue fast," Jesse replies, ignoring Storm's warning. Quickly she helps you get your wounded teammate onto the stretcher while you keep watch.

A few seconds later, Jesse pauses at the door to take one last look at the Sentinel. "I wonder if I could get a crane big enough to move that thing," she muses.

"Where would you put it?" Storm asks.

"How about Henry Gyrich's parking space?" Jesse answers with a snicker.

"Great idea!" you mutter, but you don't feel much like laughing just yet. Although you've just defeated the Sentinel, your job isn't finished until you find a way to get these people off the island safely, along with Rogue and Nightcrawler. But that will have to wait until morning. With any luck, things will look more cheerful in the sunlight. For now, your adventure has come to an end.

You try to leap aside, but you're not fast **122N**
enough to avoid the ninja's attack completely. His blade catches you in the shoulder. The wound burns like fire, and you have a terrible suspicion that the blade was poisoned. Subtract 4 from your Health points.

The ninja steps back, watching you. *If he thinks I'm going to collapse at his feet, he's got another think coming!* you think angrily. Yet you are beginning to feel dizzy, so you decide you might be better off retreating.

Make a Teleportation FEAT by rolling one die and

adding the result to your Teleportation ability. If the total is 11 or 12, turn to **105**. If it is 13 or more, turn to **80**.

123N You teleport away with the Sentinel's head, reappearing only a short distance from the torso. A fountain of sparks shoots out from the pit. Add 2 to your Karma Pool for destroying the Sentinel.

The centis bob and spin about in a frenzy of confusion, but some of the little mechanical beasts head toward you. You have just strength enough to teleport away.

Storm looks at you angrily when you reappear at her side.

"Well? Are you satisfied?" she growls.

"Perfectly," you reply. "That's one Sentinel who's going to miss the ball tonight."

"Between Wolverine's machismo and your swashbuckling, the two of you will drive me crazy yet," she continues.

"Did I hear someone mention me?" a deep voice asks from out of the darkness.

"Logan! Rogue!" Storm greets your two other teammates as Rogue lands beside you with Wolverine in her arms.

" 'Lo, darlin'," Wolverine says, smiling at Storm. "Are y'all right?" Rogue asks, setting Wolverine down gently. "Why aren't you back at the base?"

Quickly, Storm fills in Wolverine and Rogue about how the two of you got outside the mass wall. Then you relate the brief story of how you destroyed the Sentinel.

"We understand you've been hunting ninjas," you say to Wolverine.

"Yep—the Hand, to be exact. Tangled with a few of 'em, but haven't found the rest yet. Thought we should get back to you first."

"But you didn't save any dessert for us," Rogue says.

"There is still much to be done," Storm assures the girl. "Providing, of course, that Jesse can get Gyrich to let us back through the mass wall."

"Gyrich is here?" Wolverine snarls.

Storm nods wordlessly. You doubt that her calm will spread to the hot-tempered Wolverine. Turn to **17**.

124W
You make short work of the first two mechanical horrors that appear, but many more swarm over your head toward your teammates. Out of the corner of your eye, you can see them firing some sort of pencil-thin blue beams at Nightcrawler. Turn to **34**.

125R
You realize, too late, how dangerous the *metsubishi* can be when you breathe in the powder blown into your face. You are vaguely aware that Wolverine is trying to protect you from the other ninjas, but you aren't sure you're worth protecting at this point.

You start feeling incredibly dizzy, and you crash to your knees. One ninja pounces on you, his weapon upraised. As you start to lose consciousness, you think, *Ah guess invulnerability isn't all it's cracked up to be!* Your adventure is over.

126N
Holding on to Michael's shoulders, you watch as Rogue heads back toward the Sentinel. You hadn't had much success with your ninja sword anyway. You feel a little more useful protecting the boy. You know you can whisk him away from danger faster than the others by teleporting him. For now, though, you remain on the sidelines, watching the battle's progress.

Michael tries to jerk your hand away, complaining, "I want to help! I'm good with the sonic pistol!"

"I don't know how you got down here, kid," you say to Michael sternly, "but you aren't going to get anywhere near this fight. It is far too dangerous."

In the meantime, the robot, even though it's lying on its back, is far from helpless. It continues to probe the air for a victim with its giant hands. Storm, intent on shooting at the centis, doesn't see it snaking toward her until it's too late. The Sentinel grabs her in one huge hand, and she is powerless to free herself! You can see the pain on the woman's face, but she never cries out as the monster begins to crush her in its fist. Subtract 10 from Storm's Health points.

Suddenly, Michael breaks free from your grip and rushes forward, pointing his sonic pistol at the Sentinel's head.

"Let her go!" the boy shouts, firing his weapon at the Sentinel.

Certain the sonic pistol will have no more effect on the giant robot than a gnat on an elephant, you lunge for the boy, grabbing at his shirt.

To your astonishment, the Sentinel goes limp and drops Storm to the ground. Storm rolls from the monster's fist and leaps to her feet with her own sonic pistol held ready, but the Sentinel remains absolutely still. The centis hover about, as though uncertain what they should do next.

"Hey! What a great shot!" the boy shouts. "Did you see that?"

Wolverine slides off the Sentinel's chest and stares at Michael oddly.

"I wonder what *Herr* Logan is thinking," you mutter. Turn to **201**.

127W

When the Hand assassin's mind becomes absorbed by Rogue, his body slips into unconsciousness, and Rogue lets it drop to the ground. You study your partner momentarily for signs of distress, but she stands perfectly still and calm.

"Rogue? You okay?" you ask.

"I'm fine," the young woman answers, but she doesn't look fine to you. Her hands are clenched into fists, and she is breathing very hard.

"How many Hand assassins are there on the island?" you ask.

"More than enough," she replies.

Something about her answer disturbs you greatly. Make an Intuition FEAT by rolling one die and adding the result to your Intuition ability. If the total is 18 or less, turn to **152**. If it is 19 or more, turn to **40**.

128R As you grab for Gyrich, you see Storm dodge behind a control panel. You're impressed with how quickly she read the situation and sprang into action. Turn to **50**.

129W After putting away the first-aid equipment, Dr. Laughlin returns to the table where you are all seated. *Now maybe we'll get some answers about what's going on here,* you think to yourself, but you wait patiently for Storm to speak for the team. Turn to **85**.

130R *Wolverine warned me this could be dangerous,* you think as you begin to lose control of your own body. Turn to **127**.

131S You land a karate chop to Andrews's wrist, and the micro-rifle clatters to the floor. Before the scientist can bend over to recover it, you have kicked it in Michael's direction. Without picking the weapon up, the boy quickly slides a red box out of the weapon.

"Jesse threatened to hang me by my tongue if she ever caught me touching it," he explains. He tosses the red box to you. "That's the power pack. The micro-rifle's harmless now."

Turn **74**.

132S The signal leads you down the slope to a dark hole in the hillside. Suddenly, the buzz of centis comes from inside the hillside. About twenty of the strange spheres come whipping out of the ground, apparently freshly charged and ready for action.

The three of you quickly fire on them with your subsonic pistols. Bunched together as they are and at close range, they are impossible to miss. Many of them fizzle to the ground, and two explode violently, damaging all the others around them.

You tap Rogue on the shoulder and signal her to move forward. Turn to **83**.

133W

You unsheathe your claws and use them to fend off the next blow from the sword. The steel strikes so hard against the adamantium that your muscles ache, but you're reluctant to use your deadly claws against your teammate.

I've got to do something to reach Rogue before it's too late! you think desperately.

Retracting your claws, you leap toward Rogue, intent on making flesh-to-flesh contact before the ninja who controls her skewers you on his sword.

Make a Fighting FEAT by rolling one die and adding the result to your Fighting Without Claws ability. If the total is 10 or less, turn to **170**. If the total is 11 or more, turn to **44**.

134W

You hack viciously at the first line of attacking mini-robots. At least four fall at your feet, done in by your razor-sharp claws. Many more, though, swarm over your head in the direction of your teammates.

As long as those little horrors stay airborne, you realize, *it's got to be up to Rogue to deal with them.*

For now, though, you can't turn your attention from the spheres foolish enough to fly within your arms' reach. Turn to **45**.

135R

You position your body right in the center of the barrage. Shurikens of every size and shape thunk into you, but they merely bounce off harmlessly.

You crouch down beside Wolverine and Storm and whisper, "You guys all right?"

"Just fine, darlin'," Wolverine answers as he gets up, "but this is costin' us a fortune in costumes."

Your look down at your own costume. It hangs about you in tatters. "But this is the style," you tease, brushing back the lock of white hair that has fallen over your face. Turn to **57**.

136N
"I have nothing to tell Storm until I see what's on the other side," you explain. "I won't be gone for more than a few minutes. Don't worry."

Before Jesse can reply, you teleport beneath the floor. Once on the other side of the cement floor, you begin to fall downward. You must be in some sort of wide vertical shaft, for although you reach out frantically, you find nothing to grab on to.

Make an Agility FEAT by rolling one die and adding the result to your Agility ability. If the total is 12 or less, turn to **174**. If it is 13 or more, turn to **66**.

137N
Under Storm's orders, you begin to explore the entire base, but the basement reveals something so interesting that you teleport back to the control center with a startled Mrs. Taggert. "There's a hidden passage beneath the base!" you tell Storm.

"According to the maps I studied, the base was built on solid bedrock," the X-Men leader says.

"Then the maps are mistaken," you insist.

"We will check it out," Storm says.

Followed by your teammates and an angry Henry Gyrich, you hurry down the basement stairs. Jesse is there working on the mass field. She watches you curiously as you lead the others to a section of the concrete floor that is badly cracked. You tap on it once with your ninja sword. "Hear it? It's hollow underneath."

"Perhaps it is just an old well," Storm suggests.

"Or maybe a mine," Rogue adds. "Professor X said they

used t' do some mining around here."

"A cave or a mine would be the perfect place for a rogue Sentinel to hide," Wolverine points out.

"Shall I smash through, boss?" Rogue asks.

"I forbid it!" Gyrich declares. "You'll only let whatever is under there loose on this base!"

"Mr. Gyrich," Storm says tightly, "if there is a Sentinel beneath this building, even you must realize this layer of concrete is not going to stop it. The mass field is supposed to extend down through the bedrock beneath this installation. Undoubtedly, the Sentinel, if there is one, is on the other side of the mass field, or it would have gotten in here a long time ago."

Without further argument, Storm nods to Rogue.

The young mutant flies up to the basement ceiling, then plunges down, smashing the floor. She creates a hole, a meter across, through the ten inches of concrete. Warm air rises up into the basement, and you can hear wind blowing in the passages below.

Storm shines a flashlight beam down the shaft. "It appears to be about thirty feet to the bottom. The X-Men will go down to investigate. Do not follow us. Wait back at the control room. If we must go through the mass field in the passages below, Nightcrawler can teleport us to the surface in front of a security monitor so you can see us when we are ready to come back inside."

"Good luck!" Jesse calls.

"And to you," Storm replies.

You teleport Storm and Rogue flies with Wolverine down to the bottom of the shaft. A horizontal passage leads away from it. You follow the passage, creeping along as quietly as possible.

"These walls don't look like any old mine to me," Wolverine whispers. "Too round and smooth."

"No. They look as though they've been excavated by modern machinery of some sort," Storm agrees.

Sixty feet down the passage, your progress is halted when you come to a rusting steel door. It's fastened in place with an ancient padlock.

Wolverine offers to slash the door open, but Storm wants to leave at least one barrier between whatever lies beyond and the people above. "It will take only a minute to pick the lock," she insists.

While Storm is fiddling with the lock, Wolverine senses the whine of a centi approaching from behind you! Rogue shines a flashlight down the corridor as you and Wolverine aim your sonic pistols in the direction of the sound. Finally you see it in the flashlight's beam. The centi hovers in the light, moving more slowly than the others did earlier. It halts for a moment in midair, then flees back down the passage.

"Follow it!" Storm orders. "It must not make it inside into the base!"

You teleport back to the vertical shaft and wait in the darkness with your sonic pistol held ready. You can see a little spot of light moving down the passage toward you.

Make an Agility FEAT by rolling one die and adding the result to your Agility ability. If the total is 12 or less, turn to **48**. If it is 13 or more, turn to **16**.

138W

Just before you step on the wooded path that follows the shoreline, you notice several peculiar parallel lines in the sandy dirt.

"What is it?" Nightcrawler asks as you bend over to examine them.

"Footprints," you reply.

"Mighty peculiar footprints," the blue mutant comments.

"Those marks are meant to mask footprints. They're made by blades attached to the bottoms of shoes. It's an old ninja trick," you explain.

"Good. Better to fight old ninjas than young ones."

You don't crack a smile, but Kurt's attempts at levity don't go unappreciated. A group like the X-Men needs someone to lift their spirits, and the German-born acrobat's sense of irony and word play does the trick more often than not.

"Can you get us into the branches of that tree?" you ask, glancing upward.

"One sugar maple branch, coming up!" Kurt teleports both of you to a location high in the tree. You sit as still as a hunting cat. Nightcrawler crouches beside you, his tail occasionally switching slowly. After several minutes, your patience is rewarded. Two shadowy figures are moving along the edge of the beach, keeping near the forest. You catch their scent. Mikey's "shadows" are men after all.

Leaping from the tree, you land in front of them. "Hit first, ask questions later," has always been your motto in dealing with ninjas.

Make a Fighting FEAT by rolling one die and adding the result to your Fighting Without Claws ability. If the total is 10 or less, turn to **190**. If it's 11 or 12, turn to **171**. If it's 13 or more, turn to **115**.

Your flight path leads you in a zigzag pattern **139R** through the air, knocking into any mini-robots that are using laser weapons on your companions. Below, you see Storm taking advantage of the enemy's temporary disorientation. The X-Men's team leader grabs hold of a charred tree branch and smashes any attackers that come too close.

"Way to go!" you cheer.

Storm shouts up at you, "Rogue! Look out . . ."

You look up to find yourself flying directly into a sphere that is aiming a tiny metal prod at you. You can't pull up quickly enough to avoid a collision. The prod jabs at your forehead, and suddenly you can't move.

Oh, my gosh! I'm fallin'! you think as you watch Storm and the ground grow rapidly closer and closer. Turn to **157**.

140S "You'd better have your lockpicks handy," Kurt suggests. "There's a big, rusty padlock and a hot-tempered centi waiting for us below."

Almost as an afterthought, he hands you his flashlight. Then he rummages through the basement until he discovers a piece of metal sheeting. Finally he teleports the two of you from the basement to a pitch-black underground passage.

For a moment, you must fight for control. Darkness and underground places have terrified you since childhood, when you were trapped in the rubble of a bombed-out building with your mother's corpse. But you manage to win the battle against your fear. Hurriedly, you switch on the flashlight. The walls about you are bedrock, damp and cool.

"There is the lock," Nightcrawler says, pointing out a huge, aging padlock on a steel door before you.

You slip a wire pick into the keyhole and jiggle it gently, feeling out the placement of the pins. Suddenly, a high-pitched whine fills the air about you.

"Storm!" Nightcrawler whispers, "I think the centi is back!"

"I can hear him," you mutter, trying not to lose your concentration on the lock.

Make an Agility FEAT by rolling one die and adding the result to you Agility ability. If the total is 10 or less, turn to **120**. If it is 11 or more, turn to **164**.

"Why are the passages so twisty?" you ask **141R** Michael as you follow him through the maze of rooms and corridors.

"Security—to confuse possible intruders. It works, too. When Henry arrived, he got lost first thing."

"But ah thought Henry was the head of your security."

"Not really. Herb was, but when he didn't come back, Henry appointed himself. See, the government sent Henry to investigate our reports about the centis going haywire. Jesse calls him a paranoid nephew of Uncle Sam, and that's why Dr. Andrews runs and tells him everything. Dr. Andrews was hired for this project solely on the basis of his qualifications as a snitch. Jesse says Dr. Craig was hired because he's good without being imaginative."

"My, my! Jesse certainly has some interestin' opinions. What about Dr. Laughlin?"

"Dr. Laughlin's all right. He discovered me, so to speak, after I won second prize in the New York State Public School Science Fair. I would have won first, but Dr. Laughlin was the only judge there who was capable of understanding the implications of my work. He offered me this job."

"Ah see. And how did you get to be such a brilliant kid?" you ask.

Michael shrugs. "My mom taught me, mostly. She's a teacher."

"Sounds like she must be pretty good at her work."

"She's the best. But they don't pay teachers very

well, you know. So she quit so I could come and work here. I think she misses it, though."

The two of you ride up an elevator, and Michael explains, "We're on the second underground level. This is where all the laboratories are."

"What about your dad?" you ask.

Michael mumbles something you can just barely hear, but you recognize his embarrassment immediately. You've felt the same way before.

"My dad left my mom, too," you tell the boy.

Michael does not reply, but you can tell he's thinking about what you just said. He leads you into a lab and offers you a stool to sit on. As he starts pulling out equipment from cabinets and piling it on a workbench, he asks, "How did you get to be a super hero, anyway?"

"It jus' happened. Ah'm a mutant, you know." You shrug, unwilling to go into all the details.

"What else can you do besides fly?" Michael asks.

"Well, ah'm pretty strong. Ah can get hit without gettin' hurt. When ah touch people, ah absorb their minds and make them go unconscious for a little while."

"Sounds neat."

"Sometimes it is. Sometimes, though, it's awful."

"Why?"

"Ah can't control my absorbin' power. If ah touch someone's skin with mine, ah absorb him, whether ah want to or not."

"Oh. I'll bet that's why your costume isn't as sexy as Storm's."

Your eyes widen in surprise. "Just how old are you?" you ask Michael suspiciously.

"Thirteen."

"That explains it. A teen-ager. For your information, ah don't always dress like this, but ah do have to be careful, mostly so ah don't absorb my friends."

"Can you take off your gloves and help me with these wires?" Michael shows you how to do some of the simpler wiring that goes into the sonic pistols while he adjusts the frequency of the tiny amplifiers. You put three of the subsonic pistols together in about twenty minutes, then you and Michael decide to have a little fun testing them out by aiming them at an oscilloscope microphone.

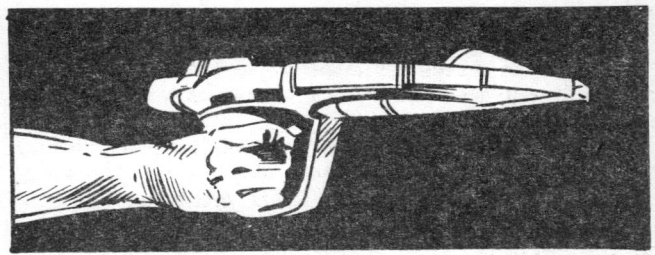

"You're a good shot," you tell Michael, a little surprised after seeing him flatten the wave signal on the oscilloscope every time he fires.

"Thanks. I must be getting better. Before we got stuck here, Jesse used to take me out to shoot cans, but I wasn't very good at it. Real guns are too heavy and loud. This is easier."

"We'd better be getting back to the control room," you suggest as you slip two of the pistols inside your belt.

You're met with a nasty surprise upon your return to the control room, however. Dr. Andrews has returned with the station's self-appointed security chief, and you discover that you know him. "Henry" proves to be none other than Henry Peter Gyrich, and as far as the X-Men are concerned, he is your sworn enemy! Turn to **179**.

I'd almost forgotten how much I enjoyed tearin' **142W**
these things to shreds, you think to yourself. In the back of your mind, though, is a brief glimpse you had of Michael firing at the centis. You suspect there is more to the boy than everyone thought.

In a short time, you and Rogue have slashed and

pounded the Sentinel into a mass of spaghetti wires and scrap metal. Storm, Michael, and Nightcrawler pick off any centis that threaten, though many of them begin to hover passively, uncertain of what to do without their leader.

"Ah think it's finally dead, Wolvie," Rogue says from beside you. The Sentinel hasn't moved for several minutes. The only sounds it makes now are the sizzling of shorted circuitry.

"I guess we should join the others," you say, sliding off the creature's chest. Turn to **201**.

143W You scout farther and farther from the scene of battle, confident that Rogue should have no problem guarding your prisoner. You both smell and see evidence that there are many more than five ninjas on the island, but you can't pinpoint exact numbers.

A scream shatters the forest's night calm. It sounds like Rogue! You race back to where you left her.

Isn't too hard to tell what happened here, you think, noting instantly that your prisoner is lying unconscious on the ground. Rogue stands beside him with one glove off, shaking like a leaf.

"Reckless kid!" you mutter. Still, it's hard to watch her in pain without feeling sympathy. Moving closer to her, you see that her cheeks are stained by tears.

You wipe away her tears with your glove. Your presence seems to snap her back to reality.

"Oh, Logan, it was awful! There was somethin' awful inside his head. It tried to take my soul! Ah know it sounds crazy, but it's true!"

"I believe you, kid," you reply, putting a comforting arm around her shoulder.

"When ah absorbed his mind, his body jus' dissolved! Something killed him for failing, and he wanted to die!"

"I tried to warn you," you say. You give her shoulders a shake. "Why do you continue to take these risks?"

"Ah don't know," she says with a shrug. "Ah guess it's kinda excitin' when it isn't awful. Ah thought we might need t' know what he knew, and ah did find out some important things."

Add 2 to your Karma Pool on Rogue's behalf for gaining control of the ninja's mind and discovering his secrets. Turn to **186**.

144S

Can we really hold these things off? you wonder, *or will they return with reinforcements?*

Already you can see the spheres that are left closing in on you, but slowly, as though they're wary of what you might do. *They probably plan to use some other weapons, like the metal bindings the first sphere used on Wolverine,* you guess.

From the top of the hill comes an unnerving grating sound. You look up, fearing to discover a fresh troop of mini-robots. On the top of the rise, though, framed by the last rays of the setting sun, is a human figure. You can just barely tell that it's a woman in a pair of army overalls as she aims some sort of gun at the mini-robots.

It's the gun making the grating noise, but it's a welcome sound after all. A few of the spheres explode, while the rest flee in all directions.

"Hurry!" the woman shouts, waving for you to follow her. "We can't stay out here. It's getting dark."

You don't take time to ask why she fears the dark. "Logan! Help me with Rogue," you order.

"There's life in the kid yet," Wolverine says, grinning.

"Mah teeth!" Rogue moans.

"Your teeth? They're all still there," you say, smiling, as Wolverine hefts her into his arms.

"But they hurt. Mah teeth are killin' me," the girl cries out. "All mah bones ache!"

"Sounds like the sphere hit her with some sort of low-frequency sonic weapon," Nightcrawler reasons. "If so, she'll recover, but she may ache for a while."

"Ah can walk by mahself," Rogue insists, so Wolverine puts her down gently but keeps a protective arm around her waist, just in case.

The four of you climb the rest of the way up the hill, where the woman waits impatiently. Just beyond the hilltop stand the burned-out skeletons of three barracks buildings. The woman leads you to the door of a fourth building that is miraculously untouched by the fire.

As your rescuer punches up a longer series of numbers on the door's electronic control panel, you take a moment to study her. She looks as if she's in her late twenties or early thirties, about your own height, with very short, brown hair and freckles. She's not a classically beautiful woman, but the health and confidence she radiates makes her exceedingly attractive.

The door slides open with a smooth *swoosh*, and you are all ushered inside.

After pushing a button on the wall to close the door and then ordering "Screen up" into an intercom, the woman turns back to greet you. "Welcome to what's left of Obar Island, otherwise known as Nerd Paradise. I'm Jesse."

"Thank you," you reply. You're a little puzzled by her apparent cheerfulness in the midst of the chaos around you. "And thank you for rescuing us."

"Anytime, friend. We can't *all* be blithering cowards," Jesse sniffs. "Follow me. The others will be surprised to see you."

Turn to **94**.

145S

Quickly, you duck behind a computer panel. Sparks shower down on you from above as the rifle shot hits the delicate electronic machinery. From your position, you can see Michael standing in the doorway, aiming a subsonic pistol, presumably at Dr. Andrews.

You're not certain what damage the weapon might cause, but you are certain that a young boy shouldn't be involved in this battle. You leap out from behind the panel and shove him to the floor behind another table.

You're too late, however. Behind you, you hear Andrews cry out in pain and the sound of the rifle hitting the floor. You rise to your feet again and see that the scientist is cradling a charred hand. As you kick the micro-rifle away from him, he backs away from you, terrified.

"You should not have done that," you tell Michael.

"The subsonic pistol didn't hurt him," Michael says. "It just fused some wires in the micro-rifle. That's what burned him. Besides, he's not in a tenth of the pain that Rogue is." Turn to **74**.

146W

As Rogue flies off into the forest, you consider calling her back, but you don't. *Wouldn't do much good at this point,* you think, following after her much more cautiously. *Besides, if I keep pulling her fat out of the fire, she'll just keep actin' reckless.*

A moment later, you have reason to reconsider your decision as a huge fireball ignites in the woods ahead of you. The explosion rocks the very earth. Taking a chance that there was only one booby trap laid in the area, you rush ahead. As you burst into a clearing drenched with a sizzling liquid, your nose is assailed by the stench of burning gasoline. The remains of a body are tied to a tree, but Rogue is nowhere to be seen.

It only takes you a few moments to discover Rogue's whereabouts. A line of broken underbrush and tree limbs mark the path of her flight from the explosion. Several yards away, you find her lying on the ground, groaning slightly.

"You all right?"

Rogue rises slowly without answering. Her costume is charred and torn, and she gasps as she straightens her back. Subtract 4 from Rogue's Health points.

"Ah'm fine," she moans.

"You're beginnin' to cost us a fortune in costumes, you know," you tease her.

She looks at you, her face looking ashen. "Ah jus'

killed that man tied to that tree!"

You shake your head. "No. I could smell him from the edge of the forest. He's been dead since last night."

"But ah heard him! Ah saw him move!" the young woman argues.

"You heard someone. They probably rigged a wire to jiggle him a bit just to draw you in closer. They were usin' his corpse as bait. Come on." Carefully, the two of you pick your way around the clearing.

Turn to **178**.

147S

You wait precious seconds to see if Rogue is coming. Suddenly, there's a tremendous crash, and Rogue's body disappears under the cave-in. Then all is silence.

"Goddess!" you whisper in shock. The sound of rolling boulders echoes through the passage.

"Yuck!" a familiar voice complains, and Rogue stumbles out of the darkness behind you, covered with dirt.

"Are you all right?" you ask.

"Ah'm feelin' pretty battered," Rogue admits, "but ah can go on."

Subtract 8 from Rogue's Health points.

"But what's worse," Rogue complains, "is that ah've got dirt in mah boots and dirt in mah clothes and dirt in mah hair and dirt in mah ears."

"You know what they say, kid," Wolverine says, grinning.

"What?" Rogue snaps crossly.

"It's a dirty job, but someone's gotta do it."

"We must hurry," you insist. "That quake could have been caused by a Sentinel."

You lead the others down the passage until you reach a massive cave. Moonlight from a shaft overhead illuminates the scene. The floor of the cave is strewn with boulders and broken stalactites. A few damaged centis lay beneath the fallen rocks.

Rogue flies up to the hole in the ceiling to investigate. In seconds, she lands back next to you. "The walls of the shaft are hot to the touch!" she reports.

"As though it's just been melted out by a Sentinel laser!" you guess.

"That could be what caused the cave-in," Wolverine says.

"Elevator up?" Rogue asks grimly.

"Yes," you reply.

The begrimed mutant takes hold of both you and Wolverine and flies up the shaft. When you get to the top of the shaft, you discover it's no more than fifty feet away from the base headquarters.

"Look!" Rogue whispers excitedly, pointing toward the base.

Approaching the building, which holds your injured friend and the scientists you've promised to protect, is a Sentinel! The robot stands over thirty feet tall, and it's trailed by at least a hundred centi-bots! The Sentinel moves slowly toward the base until it can touch the roof with its hand.

"Oh, no! The mass field must have collapsed!" you cry. "We've got to attack before the creature destroys everyone inside!"

But before you can launch into action, the Sentinel turns away from the building and lumbers away. It speaks in a booming, metallic voice. "Inner mass wall now down. This unit will proceed with primary function on the mainland. Instructing Hand to complete Project X-cellent Death—destroy all humans on Obar Island!"

"Is he talkin' to himself?" Rogue asks, confused.

"He was probably programmed to make verbal reports to his previous masters, and now, even though he's operating solo, he can't keep quiet," Wolverine guesses.

"Even with the mass field down, we have time before the Hand can attack the building. It is safe for the moment. We must destroy the Sentinel, though, before it escapes to the mainland to fulfill its primary function—destroying mutants," you say grimly.

"Right, boss," Rogue says. She flies off at full speed and slams right into the Sentinel.

Caught completely off guard, the Sentinel loses its balance and crashes to the ground. Wolverine moves in for the kill, but half the centis swarm toward him while the other half fly after Rogue.

In the meantime, the Sentinel begins to pick itself up off the ground, still babbling. "Warning! Contact with mutants! Under attack! This unit will destroy!"

Wolverine fires his sonic pistol at the centis attacking him. A number of them fizzle to the ground. Rogue, however, must have lost her weapon in the cave-in. She has only her fists to use against the creatures. They're effective, but it's slow work. You aim your own pistol at the centis attacking Rogue, but before you can fire, the younger woman takes a serious hit and falls toward the earth, unconscious! The Sentinel snatches her from the air with his giant fist. Then it begins to squeeze her in its grip!

"Mutant resistant to crushing. Will attempt alternate method of execution," the Sentinel intones.

Then, to your horror, the Sentinel fires a red beam of light out of his eyes, straight at Rogue's head!

Wolverine is too busy fending off the centis attacking him to react. With no other weapon at your disposal but the sonic pistol, you fire it at the Sentinel's head, praying that it will have some effect on the metallic monster.

Make an Agility FEAT by rolling one die and adding the result to your Agility ability. If the total is 10 or less, turn to **2**. If it is 11 or more, turn to **96**.

148R

You manage to catch Gyrich, and with your superior strength, you have no problem holding him up. Suddenly, he ceases struggling and collapses in your arms.

With a gasp, you realize that you never put your gloves back on, and now that you've touched the government agent's bare forearms, you have absorbed his mind!

Dr. Andrews, unable to fire because his boss is in the way, turns to fire at Storm, but she is no longer seated at the table. Andrews swings around, but the leader of the X-Men is nowhere in sight.

Dr. Craig has finally turned his attention away from the monitors. A flicker of amusement lights his eyes. "I think the ladies have the upper hand, Jonathan. Why don't you put down the micro-rifle before you do some serious damage?"

"Don't just sit there, Thomas!" Andrews snarls. "Do something!"

"What do you suggest?" Dr. Craig asks dryly. "I don't usually keep a supply of hand grenades in my coat pockets." He turns back to his monitors, once again uninvolved.

"Please lay down your weapon, Dr. Andrews," you say. "Ah won't hurt you."

The scientist looks with horror at the unconscious form of Henry Gyrich in your arms. Obviously, he has no reason to believe you.

"He's just unconscious. Honest!"

From the mind of Henry Gyrich, you know that Dr. Andrews is not the weapon-wielding type. He thinks weapons are too dangerous, but Gyrich, playing on Andrews's fear, convinced him it was the only way to keep you from killing someone.

"You know, if you miss," Michael says, "the blast will reflect all around and probably mess up all the computers, maybe even lowering the mass field. It may even hit you."

Dr. Andrews closes his eyes as though he's in pain. Then he drops the weapon to the floor.

Storm leaps over a control panel and scoops the rifle up. "Just slide that little red box out of it," Michael tells her, pointing to the weapon. "It's the power pack."

Storm disengages the power pack and pockets it. Then she hands the weapon back to Dr. Andrews. With a surprised look, he accepts it, only to lay it down immediately. "You—you aren't trying to destroy the base, are you?" he asks, looking frightened.

"No, Dr. Andrews," Storm replies calmly. "We came here to help you."

You lay Gyrich on a table and turn to face your leader, saying, "You may change your mind about helping them when you hear what this jerk Gyrich has been up to here." Turn to **95**.

149S In the darkness, you can feel Nightcrawler try to twist his body so that he will take the brunt of impact, making himself a shield for you, but the ground comes up too quickly. You land on your knees, while Kurt lands on his back, knocking the wind out of him.

"Goddess!" you mutter as pain shoots through your legs. You're relieved to find that you can stand up, despite the pain.

"Are you all right?" you ask your partner.

"I think I sprained my tail," Nightcrawler moans.

"Sorry about that."

Subtract 1 from both your Health points and Nightcrawler's.

You help Kurt to his feet, then the two of you brush the dirt from your costumes. Turn to **51**.

150N As you pat your team captain on the back, you notice his expression turn suddenly grim. "What is wrong, Logan?" you ask as the two of you move away from your teammates.

"I smell a fire, Kurt," Wolverine whispers. "A big one."

"The wind is coming in from the west," you note. "There's a U.S. Forest Preserve over that way. Do you think it could be a forest fire?"

Your friend shakes his head. "No. I smell traces of gasoline fumes, burning rubber, insulation, phosphorus. . . ."

"Phosphorus? You mean like in a fire bomb?"

You look toward the X-Men's leader, but Storm is speaking intently with Magneto as he herds the youngsters back inside to attend to their studies. You signal Rogue to come over to you and Wolverine.

"What can ah do for you gentlemen?" the young woman asks in her mellifluous southern drawl.

"Rogue, I want you to fly up over the lake and see if you can spot smoke," Wolverine says.

"All right," she replies, looking at you, puzzled.

You hold her back for a moment. "Just look, *Liebchen*," you say. "Don't get close. The fumes could be dangerous."

"Ah'll be real careful, Nightcrawler, shugah," Rogue replies teasingly. She runs a gloved finger up the blue fur along your arm and flashes you one of her dazzling smiles before she soars upward.

A touch of sadness creeps over you as you watch her fade into a speck in the sky. Rogue can be a charming flirt, but you know it is her only defense against the loneliness that her mutant power forces upon her. You can't imagine what it would be like to be cursed with her power, to have to avoid touching all human flesh. If she does touch someone, she steals that person's spirit for a time and causes him to lose consciousness. Rogue originally came to the X-Men for help with this precise problem, but so far, no one has been able to discover a way to control the automatic transfer.

"I used to feel sorry for myself," you tell Wolverine, "because I looked so different. But I cannot think of anything worse than Rogue's problem."

Wolverine shrugs. "She's probably better off than the rest of us."

"Surely you do not mean that," you whisper.

"Maybe not," he says, watching Rogue land lightly on the balls of her feet like an acrobat, her face flushed with the exhilaration of flying. She is still not jaded by this power, even though she uses it constantly. "The fire's on Obar Island," she announces. "Billowin' clouds o' black stuff. Y'all don't think the sparks could spread the fire over all that water, do you?"

"Probably not," Wolverine replies.

"Obar Island," you muse. "Isn't there some sort of military base there?"

"Last time ah flew over there, about a month ago," Rogue reports, "they were jus' puttin' up some buildin's and postin' it with some real unfriendly signs—all about prosecutin' trespassers an' stuff like that."

"Sounds like the army, all right," Wolverine mutters. Just to be sure, the three of you troop into the school kitchen to use the telephone. You listen as Wolverine reports the fire to the local authorities. He speaks to someone on the other end of the line for a moment, then says, "I see. Okay."

"What did they say?" you ask.

"That the situation is under control," Wolverine answers.

"Good."

"Not really," he replies, " 'cause they're lyin'."

"How do you know?" Rogue asks.

"I just do."

141

You've had experience with Wolverine's intuition before. He's not often wrong. You'd be willing to bet he was right now, too. "But why would they lie?" you ask.

"Maybe there's some sort of poisonous gas there, and they don't want t' panic the populace," Rogue guesses.

"You got a vivid imagination, kid," Wolverine states. "But I don't smell any poison. More likely, the army just doesn't wanna' breach security on the island. They'd rather let it burn into the water than bring in outsiders."

You shake your head. Wolverine once worked for the military, and he accepts such things matter-of-factly, but you are still appalled by such a destructive, secretive mentality. "Well?" you ask, "Should we consult with our fearless leader on this one?"

"Ah'll go find her," Rogue offers, and she hurries off to fetch Storm. Turn to **52**.

151W The ninja before you pauses, astonished that you're still alive.

"Never hesitate, bub!" you growl, leaping at him and knocking him off balance. You dispatch him with a quick karate chop. Rising to your feet, you turn to the beach, where you can hear your partner saying something to his mute ninja opponent. It sounds as if it's something about being unarmed.

Snatching up a sword from one of your fallen foes, you call out, "Hey, Captain Blood! Here! Catch!"

Nightcrawler catches the blade deftly by the handle and starts slashing at the ninja before him in earnest.

You watch with amusement. The ninja's style and Kurt's are completely dissimilar. The ninja keeps his strikes short and deadly, while Kurt waves his sword and swashbuckles as though he's performing for a Hollywood camera.

Despite the theatrics, the blue-furred mutant appears to be a better swordsman than his opponent. The ninja is beginning to wear down under the bizarre barrage of improvised movie script swordplay Nightcrawler is using.

"Surrender in the name of Her Majesty the Queen!" Kurt shouts dramatically. "Return the kidnapped Dauphin, or most surely you will swing from the gibbet!"

"Aren't you mixing your movie cliches?" you call from the sidelines. Exasperated, the ninja tries to beat a hasty retreat. You down him with a flying tackle, and with one quick bash, you put an end to his struggling.

"I don't think he was enjoying himself much," Kurt says, puzzled.

"Maybe he's seen that movie before," you offer.

"Critics!" Nightcrawler sniffs, tossing his head in mock arrogance. You laugh, though actually the blue mutant looks quite dashing with a sword.

Turn to **4**.

152W

Unable to pinpoint exactly what is bothering you, you begin to question Rogue in more detail. "How many ninjas are enough?" you demand.

In one smooth motion, Rogue bends over and scoops up a sword dropped by one of the ninjas, then lunges toward you.

Aghast, you instinctively raise your arm to protect yourself. The blade cuts deep into your flesh, stopped only by your adamantium-laced bones. Subtract 3 from your Health points.

Ignoring the agony spreading up your arm, you quickly try to understand what has happened. *The ninja's will must have subverted Rogue's mind. She's no longer in control of her own body!*

Turn to **133**.

153R

Veering wildly, you tackle the laser-armed spheres, sending them spinning off dizzily, providing easy targets for Wolverine's claws. At the last possible moment, you pull up and climb vertically to avoid contact with a sphere pointing a metal prod at your head.

"Ah have no idea what that nasty-lookin' thing was, but ah'm sure ah don't want to find out," you growl.

The remaining metal spheres beneath you hover for a moment as if deciding what to do next. Then they retreat the way they came, even though a majority of them are still undamaged. Feeling triumphant, you settle to the earth next to Storm. Turn to **5**.

You are are having considerable success **154W**
against the centis with the sonic pistol, when you hear
Storm shouting your name. Whirling about, you see
she is firing her sonic pistol at the Sentinel.

What's she doing? you wonder. *That's like trying to take out Godzilla with a can of Raid.*

Then you catch a glimpse of what the Sentinel grasps in his hand. It's Rogue! The monster is frying her head with a red beam!

You break through the centis, tossing the sonic pistol aside. You unsheathe your claws as you leap toward the giant robot, slashing at its ankles in rage.

Make a Fighting FEAT by rolling one die and adding the result to your Fighting With Claws Ability. If the total is 19 or less, turn to **106**. If it is 20 or more, turn to **20**.

With a stunned look on her face, Rogue lets **155N**
you take the ball from her cupped hands. Quickly, you teleport the ball to a burnt-out section of the island, drop it, and teleport back to the boat. You've no sooner returned than you hear the sound of an explosion.

"Nice catch!" you congratulate Rogue on your return.

"Wow!" Michael whispers, wide-eyed.

"Ah think mah heart just stopped," Rogue says.

"Way to go, elf," Wolverine whispers as you collapse wearily beside him in the back of the *Lilandra*. Turn to **61**.

The shaft above you appears to be about ten **156N**
feet in diameter and rises straight up for thirty feet. To one side lies a horizontal passage about the same size. You follow the passage carefully, searching the walls and floors for signs of anything that might be down here. The tunnel ends after sixty feet at a steel door, held shut by a rusting padlock.

Suddenly, from behind you, you hear the high-pitched whine of a centi-bot! Spinning about, you catch sight of it in the beam of the flashlight. It seems to be moving more slowly than the others were. *Perhaps its batteries are low,* you think, remembering that the strange spheres are recharged by light, something at a premium in this dark corridor. Still, you have no idea what fiendish weapon it might have ready to use on you. Frantic, you begin to smash at the padlock with the back of the flashlight, but this does more damage to the aluminum light than to the iron lock. When the centi-bot is within ten feet, it fires, using the same tiny blue light you saw earlier in the evening. Subtract 3 from your Health Points.

I think I've learned enough! you mutter and teleport away. In moments, you are standing once again in front of Jesse.

"What happened?" she asks anxiously.

"I ran into a centi. It was just one, but it shot those *verdammen* blue rays at me."

"Now you know how a piece of microwave popcorn feels," Jesse says.

"What do you mean?" you ask.

"The beam fries the blood in the capillaries close to the surface of your skin. The beam breaks up every few seconds, so it doesn't do too much damage. If you took a hit that lasted a minute or more, you'd be a Thanksgiving turkey."

"That is fiendish! Did you invent this weapon?"

"I'm afraid so," Jesse replies ruefully. "Can I make it up to you by fixing up some icepacks for you?"

"Personally, I prefer the kiss-it-and-make-it-better method," you explain. Turn to **18**.

Your warning to Rogue has come too late. **157S**
The sphere's prod hits the younger woman's head, and her face contorts in pain. You watch in horror as the supposedly invulnerable mutant freezes in midair and begins falling, apparently too stunned to fly. A moment later, she crumples to the ground with a sickening thud. Subtract 3 from Rogue's Health points.

Goddess! What sort of weapon could harm Rogue? you wonder. Intent on protecting her, you leap to her side, brandishing your makeshift weapon to keep the robots at bay. Turn to **144**.

Nightcrawler teleports the two of you just **158W**
above the beach, and you fall softly onto the cool sand. The moon is nearly full, but the sky has turned cloudy, so that one moment, you can see quite clearly, and the next, all about you is shadow.

Nightcrawler looks up at the shining silver sphere. "No offense, *mein Freund*, but you are not exactly my first pick for a stroll along a moonlit beach."

You chuckle. "Trust me, pal. You wouldn't want to bring anyone you really like to this place."

"You sense danger?" Nightcrawler asks.

You take a deep breath. The breeze coming off the lake freshens the otherwise fire-scorched air. It also keeps you from picking up any human scents that might be on the island, so you can't tell what has made you feel uneasy. "I sense evil."

"Interesting. Why did you pick this place to start?" Kurt asks.

"If there are other people here, this'd be a likely place for them to have landed, to avoid being seen. If they're smart, they've got a guard watching the docks to see who else arrives."

"Shall we have a word with this person, assuming he exists?" your partner asks.

"Yeah. Let's." You walk along the beach toward the wooded path following the shoreline.

Make an Intuition FEAT by rolling one die and adding the result to your Intuition ability. If the total is 19 or less, turn to **35**. If it is 20 or more, turn to **138**.

159W
There's something wrong with Rogue, but you can't quite put your finger on it. *Maybe she's showin' signs of shock from all the ugliness she's seen today,* you guess mentally.

You turn around to pick up a robe from one of the dissolved bodies to cover Rogue's tattered costume. A peculiar feeling comes over you, and the hairs on your neck prickle. You spin about suddenly, just in time to see Rogue slash down at you with one of the ninjas' swords!

You raise your arm to fend off the blow from your neck, and the blade cuts deep into your flesh, stopped only by your adamantium-laced bone. Subtract 3 from your Health points.

How could I be so stupid? you berate yourself through the searing pain. *She's not Rogue; she's one of the Hand now. She's movin' just like a ninja—must have tried to absorb him while I was scoutin' around, only his will was greater and he took over.* Turn to **133**.

Your breath quickens as you try to hold your- **160R**
self back from turning Gyrich into hamburger. You feel
guilty enough about what you did to Ms. Marvel without
having it thrown in your face by slime like Gyrich.

"And who knows who else's powers *you* have stolen,
Mr. Gyrich," Storm says softly, reminding the government agent that he was responsible for her loss of
powers. The leader of the X-Men puts a comforting arm
around your shoulder. "Ignore him, child. He is a fool."

Under Storm's comforting touch, the need you feel to
smash something gradually subsides.

The scientists all shift uneasily away from Gyrich.
Not even Dr. Andrews will look at him. The last of the
government agent's esteem fades before Storm's calm
manner. He has lost control of the group completely.

"We are leaving this base, Mr. Gyrich," Storm
declares. "You will have to be satisfied with trying to
protect the base with the mass field. As soon as Dr.
Kirsch has constructed a remote control switch, we will
leave. Wolverine was right—we should take advantage
of the dark to make our escape. We will meet by the
mass field and step out one by one so Nightcrawler can
teleport us to the boats."

For once, Gyrich seems out of arguments. "I'm going
to change my clothes," he mutters.

Ah wish ah had Storm's way with people, you think,
watching Gyrich shuffle off in defeat. Turn to **102**.

"Allow me," you reply, scooping Jesse up in **161N**
your arms and teleporting the two of you to the doorway where you entered the complex.

You arrive with the usual *bamf* sound and Jesse looks
around, her eyes wide with astonishment. "Hey! that
was terrific!"

She is so impressed by the experience that she does
not even seem to notice the brimstone stench that
always accompanies the use of your power. "Michael
will just die of jealousy!" she declares.

You put her down gently. "I take it Michael is some sort of child genius?"

"Well, he might be. Leona, his mother, won't let them administer any I.Q. tests on him. She thinks the tests are wicked. But the things he can do with two wires and a battery make the people at Los Alamos nervous for their jobs."

Jesse begins leading you through the corridors of the ground level, which contains the offices and living quarters of the missing security personnel. As you walk, she continues to tell you about Michael. "Gerald—Dr. Laughlin—discovered Michael at a state science fair and took him under his wing. The kid has gone to inner city schools all his life, and Leona taught in them.

"When Gerald offered Michael a job out in the country that paid three times his mother's salary, they both jumped at it. Gerald is a dear man, but he missed the point entirely," Jesse says with a sigh.

"And what point is that?" you ask.

"The miracle isn't that Michael learned all about cyber-neuronics. The miracle is that Leona taught him."

"So why isn't she the one who is making all that money?"

Jesse shrugs. "No one else seems to have figured out her role. She keeps real quiet. Leona doesn't seem terribly interested in research on her own, but once something has been explained to her, she can teach it to anyone—even Jonathan."

"You are not very friendly with Dr. Andrews, are you?" you note.

"Andrews hasn't had an original idea in his life. He's a snitch for the government. I've worked with him on a few other jobs. He's got all the right degrees, but his real job is to squeal on dissidents and slackers."

"And that's why he went to report us to your security chief?" you ask.

"He went to report us to Henry. Henry's not really our security chief—just some government bigwig who came out for an inspection and got trapped here with us. When our security team disappeared, Henry just appointed himself security chief. His only qualification as a security chief is his paranoia."

"And Dr. Craig?" you ask, remembering the scientist who seemed to ignore everyone around him.

"Oh. Thomas is okay, I guess. At least he's very competent, but he has a rather limited imagination. He's not very interested in tackling the impossible."

"But you always do five impossible things before breakfast," you tease.

"Hey, why settle for greatness when you can be totally cosmic?" Jesse jokes, gesturing wildly with her hands.

"Well, it's certainly helpful having the inside dirt on everyone," you say.

Jesse leads you down a staircase to the first underground level, which houses administrative offices, and then the second, which holds the laboratories. Finally you find yourself once more on the third level, with the scientists' living quarters and the control room.

"Everything was built deliberately to resemble a maze in order to confuse intruders," Jesse tells you.

"It works," you reply, realizing that though you can teleport to anyplace in the complex that you've seen, you would probably get lost if you tried to find it on your own.

"Let's take a look at the basement," you suggest, peering down the last staircase. Turn to **100**.

"Somethin' wrong, pal?" you ask after **162W** Nightcrawler teleports the two of you away from the scene of your battle. You sheathe your claws, feeling more than a little annoyed at being dragged away from a fight.

At that moment, your partner collapses at your feet. Alarmed, you search for his pulse. It's weak, and his breathing is very shallow. You press your hand against his bleeding shoulder. "Hang in there, Kurt!" you whisper.

You lift your teammate in your arms and start toward the base. Either someone in the control room has seen you coming or the mass field has failed, because you meet no resistance as you approach the building. When you reach the door, though, you realize that you have no idea how to open it. You put Kurt down carefully, planning to use your claws to open the door when the scent of another person reaches your nostrils.

You whirl around to see another ninja springing out of the darkness, coming straight at you!

You are prepared to meet his charge, when from the doorway, Storm's sharp voice commands, "Wolverine, no!"

You freeze, then break into a grin as the charging ninja bounces backward, repelled by the mass field.

"Nice timin', darlin'!" you say to Storm.

"The skill is Dr. Kirsch's. What happened to Nightcrawler?" she asks anxiously.

"I think the ninja sword that cut his shoulder was poisoned."

You lift Kurt back into your arms gingerly and carry him inside. Michael is waiting for you with a cot on wheels.

"Dr. Craig is waiting in the infirmary for us," Storm says.

You reach the infirmary within minutes, with Michael leading the way through the tangle of corridors as you and Storm push the cart.

Dr. Craig immediately starts hooking Nightcrawler up to several incomprehensible machines, aided by Mrs. Taggert.

"Do you know what you're doin'?" you growl. "Aren't you a physicist?"

"Wolverine, Dr. Craig has a degree in medicine as well," Storm explains.

"Then why isn't he practicin' as a doctor, instead of staying holed up in this ninja rat trap?" you snap.

Dr. Craig looks up at you disdainfully. "Because I don't like boorish people," he answers. "Now, get out of here. You're not sterile."

Storm pulls you out of the infirmary. "I know Kurt is your friend, but there is nothing more you can do for him now. Let the doctor do his part."

You pace angrily in the hallway, telling Storm all that happened. "These weren't just any ninja," you conclude. "They were the Hand."

"The same assassins you fought in Japan?" Storm asks.

"Yeah."

"Your friend Yukio told me that they are not real men," Storm says.

"Oh, they're real enough, but they fight like the devil—or perhaps for the devil. It's hard to say which. And they fight dirty. There's only two reasons they might be here. Either they think there's something here they need to further their schemes of world domination, or they've been hired to kill these people."

"Or both," Storm points out.

"Yeah. Boy, when we stick our nose in other people's business, we don't mess around, do we?"

Mrs. Taggert sticks her head out of the infirmary door. "You can come in now."

With a feeling of great relief, you see Kurt sitting up in bed, his eyes open. Mrs. Taggert is seated at his side, taking his pulse.

"Sorry to drag you away from your fun," he says, smiling weakly.

"Just don't make a habit of it," you grumble teasingly. "How you feelin', pal?" you ask more seriously.

"Ready to get back into action," he answers.

Ororo looks over toward Dr. Craig doubtfully. The physician-physicist turns from the sink as he dries his hands. "If that man tries to stand up before a week goes by, he'll wind up back on the floor. Management doesn't take responsibility for patients who do not take care of themselves." With that, Dr. Craig breezes out of the room.

"Please rest, Kurt," Storm urges. "I need you well, not dead. We will come back a little later. I will need you to man the control center then."

"*Ja,*" Nightcrawler sighs. "I will do as you ask."

"You'd better," you growl, "or I'll have to sit on you!"

"Wolverine?" Kurt calls as you turn to leave with Storm.

"Yeah?"

"Thanks."

"For you, elf, anytime." You turn to follow Storm down the corridor, anxious to see what action she'll take. Turn to **46**.

163W
As though it were an aluminum can, Rogue crumbles the sphere with her bare hands. The tendrils around your wrists go limp, and the strange sphere falls to the ground.

You rub the circulation back into your hands with a feeling of relief. Though you've regenerated skin in record time, self-healed massive internal wounds that would have killed an ordinary man, and even grown fresh nerve tissue, you doubt very much that your body could grow new hands.

"Thanks, kid," you say, smiling at Rogue.

"Anytime, shugah."

Because Rogue destroyed the sphere before it could harm you, add 2 to your Karma Pool on her behalf, then turn to **89**.

164N
"This is a bad time to lose your touch, thief," you say to Storm.

"An even worse time to lose one's patience," the woman replies evenly.

How can Storm stay so calm? you think. Turn to **58**.

165R
You swoop toward Michael as fast as an eagle swooping over a rabbit, but the Sentinel is faster still. The gigantic robot snatches Michael up from the ground. You curse as you swerve to fly at the Sentinel.

Below you, you spot Wolverine leaping from the robot's chest onto the metal hand that holds the boy. Turn to **26**.

166S
"It does not matter what the voice sounded like, Logan," you insist. "We are in enough trouble with the authorities already. If we are fortunate, paperwork on the incidents involving the SHIELD helicarrier and NORAD have been shuffled to the bottom of the pile, but trespassing on a U.S. Army base will only reopen old wounds."

Rogue sighs with disappointment. You can see she'd been looking forward to a little action. Turn to **99**.

167W
You leave Rogue behind with the prisoner, confident that she can hold on to him. The paths ahead are full of booby traps, which you dodge around expertly, but the going is slow. You detect the scent of other Hand assassins, but not their exact number. The trail has shown a lot of recent use.

They must have a base around here somewhere. Maybe Rogue can spot it from the air. At any rate, I'd better get back before she starts to worry, you think.

Rogue is still standing where you left her, prisoner in hand. "Find anything?" she asks.

"Lots of traps and signs of more Hand assassins. I'd love to know exactly how many are left and where they swarm."

"This one hasn't said a word. You want me to pull it out of him?" Rogue asks.

You glance at Rogue's prisoner and consider the young woman's offer. You don't like the idea of her absorbing the mind of someone like the man in front of you. Though Rogue was once a villainess herself, and you haven't yet forgiven her for stealing Ms. Marvel's powers, you don't want any harm to befall her. Absorbing the Hand's mind could be traumatic for her.

Yet, your prisoner's information could be very useful.

It might mean the difference between getting the scientists off the island safely or not.

If you think it's too dangerous for Rogue to use her absorption power on your prisoner, turn to **36**. If you think the information to be gained is worth the risk, turn to **184**.

"Wolverine!" Storm whispers warningly. **168W**
"Remember, we are guests here!"

"Yes," Jesse agrees. "Jonathan, you really are an incredibly poor host." The woman steps up to Jonathan and gently pulls him away from you. He has turned very pale, transfixed by the three adamantium daggers you waved in his face.

Without further comment, you retract your claws. One of the other men steps forward, the eldest of the bunch, at least fifty years old with white hair and an old-fashioned bow tie. He doesn't seem to show the least hint of fear, nor is he overconfident. He reminds you of Professor Xavier; both men carry an aura of civilization that affects everyone around them.

"Welcome to Obar Island. I'm Dr. Gerald Laughlin, director of this research facility, such as it is." You move aside for Ororo to step forward. She deals better with strangers than you do, another reason she is the leader.

"I am called Storm," she explains, accepting Dr. Laughlin's outstretched hand. "And this is Rogue, Nightcrawler, and Wolverine. Please excuse us for trespassing, but we saw the fire and thought you might need help."

"Very decent of you." Dr. Laughlin smiles. "You've already met Dr. Kirsch." He nods toward Jesse. "And this is Dr. Thomas Craig." Dr. Laughlin points to a man seated at a security monitor. Dr. Craig holds up a hand in silent greeting, then turns back to the viewing screen, apparently no longer interested in your presence.

"And this is Dr. Jonathan Andrews," Dr. Laughlin continues. Andrews merely scowls at you. "You must forgive Jonathan's ungracious welcome, but our security chief's instructions were quite explicit—we were not to lower the shield for any reason."

He looks pointedly at Jesse and says, "Dr. Kirsch's sense of humanity, however, is rather stronger than her discipline. And she is inclined to take advantage of Michael's youthful judgment."

"I weighed the decision carefully," Michael protests. "I wouldn't have lowered the screen if I hadn't thought it was the correct thing to do."

You take a more careful look at the boy standing behind you. Although he looks like an ordinary, short, skinny kid, he speaks better than most adults, with perfect enunciation and a good deal of conviction.

Dr. Laughlin smiles fondly at the boy without comment.

"Meet Michael Taggert and his mother, Mrs. Leona Taggert," he concludes, indicating the other woman in the room with a nod of his head.

Storm nods at each of the adults, smiling warmly at Michael, who is now standing beside you and observing you as carefully as you studied him. "You are also a member of the team?" Storm asks Michael.

"Yes, ma'am," Michael says, nodding, "specializing in cyber-neuronics."

"Cyber-what?" Rogue asks.

"Cyber-neuronics. Simply put," Michael explains, "it is the study of the actions and reactions of people and things programmed to behave as people—how and why they do what they do."

"Things programmed to act like people?" Nightcrawler asks.

"The centi-bots," Jesse explains.

You mean those flamin' little monsters outside that tried to kill us?" you ask indignantly. "You programmed them?"

"Well, yes, but not to kill people," Michael protests. "We programmed them to serve as guards. Later we hoped to program them for high-risk services."

"Burning buildings, cave-ins, maybe even hostage

situations," Jesse explains. "The centi-bots can get into tight places, and they're well armed and armored, but ultimately expendable. A few days ago, though, they started to malfunction."

"Either the group dynamics subroutines are confusing them, or else they're being reprogrammed somehow," Michael adds.

"They didn't look confused to me," you mutter.

"Reprogramming is impossible," Dr. Craig mutters without turning around from his viewing station.

"No, it isn't!" both Jesse and Michael reply at the same time.

"Enough!" Dr. Laughlin reprimands. "Let's save that discussion for later. Why don't we make our guests more comfortable before we delve any deeper into our story?" he suggests.

If any members of your team took damage in the battle with the centi-bots, turn to **76**. If no one lost any Health points, turn to **49**.

Your reactions aren't quite fast enough. The missile lands in the boat alongside yours and rolls to the other side.

169R

"I've got it!" Michael shouts excitedly, picking up the ball. But instead of tossing it overboard, he merely stands there, studying it.

"Throw it away, Michael!" you scream desperately. "Throw it in the water!"

Mrs. Taggert knocks the ball out of her son's hands, but in doing so, she slips and falls on the deck. The missile falls toward the water.

Too surprised to duck for cover, Michael stands at the

boat rail watching the weapon descend toward the water.

The explosion slams him clear across the boat, where he collapses to the deck. Nightcrawler leaps across to the other boat and kneels at the boy's side. "He is still breathing, " he says, "but his burns are serious."

"Nightcrawler, are you strong enough to get him to the hospital at Salem Center?" Storm asks.

"I can handle it," Kurt assures her. Quickly, he scoops up the injured boy and teleports away.

"My baby!" Mrs. Taggert cries out.

"The sooner your son receives treatment, the better, Mrs. Taggert," Storm calms her. "We'll take you to Michael as soon as we land."

It's a subdued and exhausted group that pulls up to the Salem Center boat docks fifteen minutes later. A U.S. Army bus and motorcade are waiting there, thanks to Henry Gyrich. The scientists all ignore Gyrich's efforts to herd them aboard the bus. With you blocking the soldiers, there is nothing the government agent can do to keep everyone from accompanying the pale Mrs. Taggert to the hospital.

Nightcrawler is waiting for you outside the hospital's intensive care unit, looking haggard. All the teleporting he has done today has been quite a strain on him.

"Your son will be all right," he tells Michael's mother. "He'll be scarred, but his life is in no danger."

Leona Taggert's self-control slips away. She starts to weep with relief.

"He's groggy from what they've given him for the pain, but he'll recognize you," Nightcrawler adds.

Several minutes later, Mrs. Taggert emerges from the intensive care unit and heads straight for Storm.

"Michael says he'd like to say good-bye to the X-Men before he's transferred to another hospital."

"Of course," Storm answers. In moments, the four of you are gathered around Michael's bed.

"I guess it was pretty stupid of me to hold on to that ball, huh?" he asks you.

You shrug. "Ah do that sort of thing all the time, Michael, only ah'm invulnerable."

"That must be neat," the boy says. "And to teleport like you do, Nightcrawler. Mom said you saved my life by getting me here so fast. Thank you." Then shyly he asks Wolverine, "Would you do that thing with your claws just once more?"

A little self-consciously, Wolverine extends the three adamantium claws on his right hand.

"Neat!" Michael whispers. "It was swell to meet all of you. I hope we meet again someday." His voice trails off, and you can see that he is falling asleep under the influence of the sedatives.

"I hope we meet again, too, Michael," Storm whispers. "Until then, farewell."

As you turn to leave, you know that, whether you ever see Michael again or not, you will never be able to forget him. And you swear that someday you will make the Hand pay for what they did to him. Your adventure is over.

170W

You duck in under the samurai blade and wrestle Rogue to the ground, hoping to land with your face close to hers. When instead you land with your face far from hers, you realize you are unable to force her to absorb your mind. The ninja in Rogue's body places you in a crushing hold, as though it's just becoming aware of the girl's great strength.

You feel your ribs cracking and the air being forced out of your lungs. As your sight begins to dim, you realize that you must stop Rogue somehow. There's no telling if and when the ninja will leave her mind, and in Rogue's body, he can easily get past the mass field around the research base.

With your fist pressed up against Rogue's throat, you send the mental command to your claws to extend just as you begin to black out. Your last hope is that Storm and Nightcrawler will succeed where you and Rogue have failed. This is the end.

171W Your fist slams into one ninja's chest, sending him crashing into a bush. Then you turn to deal with the second one. He lunges at you with his sword drawn. Unsheathing your claws, you parry his strike and slash at his arm. The ninja backs off, but you know it's a ploy—you can smell the first one sneaking up behind you.

You slam your foot into the ninja behind you, and he makes a highly improbable second visit to the bush he just pulled himself out of. Temporarily distracted, you lose sight of the ninja with the sword, until you feel the blade slice into your shoulder.

Make a Fast Healing FEAT by rolling one die and adding the result to your Fast Healing ability. If the total is 21 or 22, turn to **65**. If it is 23 or more, turn to **88**.

172W With your free hand, you hack at the other ninja's sword. The force and angle of your blow sends your opponent's weapon sailing from his hand.

From his other hand, the red-clad assassin releases a shuriken into your forearm. The tiny weapon draws blood, but you neither smell nor feel any poison in the wound, and you know the cut will heal within a few minutes. Turn to **3**.

173W You can feel your body heating up, burning off the poison that is now shooting through it. Though you still feel the pain, it doesn't increase or spread beyond your arm, but below the constricting bindings, your hands are beginning to feel numb.

Fortunately, after blinking for several moments, Rogue recovers from her blindness and reaches out to grab the sphere once more. Turn to **56**.

174N Before there's even time to consider teleporting yourself to safety, you slam into the bottom of the shaft. You almost manage to land on your feet, but your right foot twists on a sharp rock and you collapse to the ground, silently cursing your luck. Subtract 1 from your Health points and turn to **156**.

175S Just as you are about to duck behind a computer console, the rifle beam hits you square in the back. You feel as though you've been hit by a truck. Your lungs are on fire! You aren't aware of anything but the pain for a long time. When it begins to subside, you find yourself looking up at Rogue. Her face is covered with tears.

"Storm! Thank heavens you're alive! Michael says you shouldn't try to move. Just lie right there and rest. Ah'll take care of everything. Wolverine and Nightcrawler should be back soon, and then we'll get you home."

"Good girl," you whisper. You're glad Rogue is going to handle things, because you are too tired to even think. You drift back into a dreamless sleep, uncertain of how seriously you are hurt or of what will happen to your mission now. Your adventure has ended.

176S "If I were a centi-bot, surely I'd have more than one guard in the passage," you reason aloud. "And surely I'd think of a way to attack the base from the basement. Why haven't they?"

You're sure that the answers to these questions are

important. "Of course!" you exclaim. "Kurt, according to the maps in the control center, the mass field covers the base, but it also goes straight into the ground. We're near the edge of the base, so we're also near the mass field. The centis can't get past because the mass field is between us and the pit!"

Nightcrawler nods excitedly and points to a group of centis. Every few moments, one appears to bounce off an invisible wall.

"That's why there's only one guard in the corridors," you explain. "All the other centis were on the other side of the room when the mass field went up!"

"Or they drifted across the mass field afterward and can't get back," Kurt adds.

"If we try to get close enough to look inside the pit, we'll be stuck outside the field. Logically, I should be the one to go," you state.

"Why?"

"You can teleport back upstairs from here. I cannot. I can find the way out used by the centis and signal Jesse from a camera on the outside."

"I've got a better idea. I'll go with you."

"There is no sense in risking both our necks," you object.

"Except that two heads are better than one," Nightcrawler retorts. "Look, if you sneak over to that exit," he suggests, pointing to a passageway on the far side of the room, "I'll teleport up to that ledge and have a look inside the pit, then teleport back and meet you at the door. Then we can search for the way out. If things get too rough, we can teleport outside the base."

You can find no flaw with Kurt's plan, except that it will leave you both outside the protection of the mass wall, completely dependent on Jesse to get back in. But you have a feeling that you can rely on her, so you nod in agreement.

Kurt gives you a head start, and you begin to slip around the edges of the cave. Fortunately, it's darker near the outside of the room, and the centis are concentrating on whatever they're doing in the pit. You feel nothing unusual as you pass through the mass wall, but you can tell it's there by the centis, who occasionally bump into it and rebound off.

You watch Kurt teleport to the ledge above the pit as planned. Then something goes wrong. From the pit, a metallic voice booms, "Warning—mutant in vicinity! Identification: Nightcrawler. Capture immediately!"

Kurt teleports to your side with a stunned look on his face. Turn to **110**.

177W

You use your claws to keep yourself from sliding off the metal armor that covers the Sentinel. You are just about to step on a metal grid, but something about it seems dangerous. You push down on it with one claw, then pull your hand back quickly. A red beam of light shoots out from the grid. You aren't about to try to find out what it does. No doubt it's something deadly.

Carefully, you skirt around the red beam and slide down into the Sentinel's throat. You hack at its neck and head until it finally stops its warning cry.

It lies perfectly still. The centis hover aimlessly for a moment, then float to the ground, apparently no longer hostile. You take that as a good indication that the Sentinel is dead.

You slide off of the giant robot to join Storm, who is kneeling beside Rogue's body. Turn to **121**.

178W

"Ah might have killed that man if he hadn't already been dead," Rogue says quietly.

"Learn from that lesson, kid, and be more careful in the future," you tell her. "But don't dwell on it. Death was probably a release for him, anyway."

"What do you mean?"

"From the uniform he's wearing, I'd say he was one of the missing guards. The Hand would have only one reason to keep him as a prisoner," you explain. "They'd want to know how many people are inside the base, and how to get through the mass-field wall. That's probably why they blew up the generator last night."

"You—you mean they tortured him?" Rogue chokes.

You nod, then dismiss the subject. Rogue looks pale, and you know it's not just the moonlight. *As tough as she acts, she's really got a pretty tender heart,* you think. *This is a lousy job for a teen-ager.*

Still, the girl follows gamely behind you, determined to get even with the assassins, as you continue tracking the man whose trail has led you this far.

You can hear as well as smell him now. From the way he stops occasionally and waits, you guess that he knows you are following him. You suspect he may even be leading you into an ambush.

I wonder if he knows that I know he knows, you think. *That would make the game more deadly.*

Your quarry's scent mingles with that of four other men. You've been told that Hand assassins often travel and attack in fives.

"We've got a full house," you whisper to Rogue. "Let's blitzkrieg 'em. Thataway!"

Rogue gets a good grip beneath your arms and flies off with you. You don't see the ambush ahead, but you know it's there, waiting. Letting your intuition guide you, you soar over the brush until you see the slightest flicker of a shadow. Then you signal Rogue to drop you to the ground below.

Your fall causes a small disturbance in the brush, but the shadowy shape that moves toward you, sword

drawn, is unprepared for your sudden appearance. With a perfectly placed kick and a second blow with the side of your hand, you put your attacker out of commission, then quickly check out your foe. He wears the red robes of the Hand, and he's armed to the teeth with weapons only a ninja would use.

You hear a disturbance several yards away and realize that Rogue has made her first strike. You sneak up on the noise until you can see what's going on. Rogue has knocked out another assassin. He lies slumped against a tree. In the close quarters of the forest, though, your partner can hardly keep taking off and dive-bombing her targets, so she remains on the ground, trying to land a blow on a third and fourth ninja. With her strength, one blow is all she'll need, but the Hand assassins are agile and dodge her punches and kicks expertly.

As you watch, Rogue's attackers discover that their shurikens merely bounce off her and that their shortswords, which have shredded her costume, haven't even nicked her.

You are reluctant to reveal your position until you see the fifth assassin, but one of the ninjas pulls out a small weapon that you know could spell trouble for the young woman.

The device is a *metsubishi*, a small box with a mouthpiece and a blowhole. Customarily, it's loaded with dust or powdered pepper, which can be blown into an opponent's face. Knowing the Hand as you do, however, you'd be willing to bet this *metsubishi* contains something more deadly. Rogue's skin may be thick, but her lungs are vulnerable, and you must act immediately.

You launch yourself at the assassin aiming the weapon at Rogue. To keep him from maneuvering in close enough to harm her, you must make a Fighting FEAT by rolling one die and adding the result to your Fighting Without Claws ability. If the total is 10 or less, turn to **188**. If it is 11 or 12, turn to **55**. If it is 13 or more, turn to **180**.

179R You have had contacts—unpleasant ones—with Henry Gyrich before. If Gyrich had his way, all mutants—the good along with the bad—would be rounded up and forced to live in internment camps. What makes him so dangerous, though, is the power he wields as a member of the National Security Council. He once tried to neutralize your mutant abilities, but by accident, he hit Storm instead, leaving her with only her human skills and talents. You felt guilty about Storm's loss on your behalf, but Gyrich apparently never suffered a twinge of remorse.

Dr. Craig seems completely oblivious to the scene, staring at the monitors as though no one else were about. Mrs. Taggert is nowhere in sight. Dr. Andrews is holding some sort of huge, modern rifle. Storm is seated at a table, with Gyrich standing beside her. His jacket is off, revealing a shoulder holster containing a revolver. When Dr. Andrews sees you, he swings the rifle around to point it at you.

Your teammate doesn't seem the least bit worried, however. As a matter of fact, Storm looks somewhat amused by this petty dictator. Gyrich is obviously overheated. He has his sleeves rolled up, and sweat beads on his forehead.

"Glad to see you could join us, Rogue," the government agent says with a sneer. "By the way, you are under arrest for trespassing on government property. Maybe later we'll be able to tack on some of the older outstanding charges against you. Where is Dr. Kirsch?"

You have to laugh at his audacity. "Why should I tell you, Gyrich?"

"Dr. Kirsch is on report. She and Michael Taggert are both to be confined to their quarters so they won't make any more trouble."

"You mean so they can't let Wolverine and Nightcrawler back inside," you say. "Don't you realize that we came out here to help you, you jerk?"

"We don't need any help from mutants!" Gyrich growls. "Now, sit down. The weapon Dr. Andrews holds will damage even you. I guarantee it. Michael, your mother is waiting for you in your room."

"I'm going to go tell Jesse that you've got her microrifle!" Michael says, "Boy, are you gonna get it!"

Gyrich circles around you to move toward the door and escort Michael out of the control room, but the boy tenses defensively. Then, with a sudden burst of ferocity, he pushes Gyrich straight at you, shouting, "Here, Rogue! Catch!"

Gyrich stumbles toward you, and you instinctively reach out to grab him. It occurs to you that he might make a good shield against the weapon Dr. Andrews holds.

You must make a Strength FEAT by rolling one die and adding the result to your Strength ability. If the total is 13 or less, turn to **128**. If it's 14 or more, turn to **148**.

180W

You spring from the undergrowth, slamming the ninja into a tree before he can blow through the deadly *metsubishi*.

"Whoa!" Rogue cries out, startled by your action. *She has no idea that I may have just saved her skin,* you think, giving the stunned ninja another punch for good measure. Turn to **198**.

181S

As much as you despise Gyrich and the fascist control he wants to exert over mutants, you understand that, as far as he is concerned, he is only doing his duty. After all, he is responsible for the centi project and the research base. There is valuable equipment here that can't be carried away but can't be allowed to fall into the possession of the Hand, either.

"We could leave the base protected behind the inner mass field and lower only the outer one to escape. Then the base would be safe from intrusion," you suggest. "Would that satisfy you, Mr. Gyrich?"

Gyrich looks at you, surprised that you've even considered his side of things. "It would keep the Hand out," Gyrich replies, "but then we wouldn't be able to get back in."

"Surely Dr. Kirsch could set the field on a timer so that it will shut off sometime in the future when you've returned with reinforcements."

"I can do better than that," Jesse says emphatically. "I can set up a radio receiver so it will shut off by remote control."

"Radio signals can pass through the mass wall?" Nightcrawler asks.

"Of course," you say, thinking rapidly. "Otherwise the security screens would not be able to monitor outside the field."

"But the mass wall could collapse and let in the Hand," Gyrich objects. "We cannot risk letting assassins get their hands on the technology in this building."

"I don't think the field is in any more danger of collapsing," you reply. "We've destroyed the Sentinel."

"So?" Gyrich asks dully.

"The Sentinel can send out signals along all sorts of wave lengths. It must have used this ability to get at your computer, to try to make it shut down the mass field."

"That's pure speculation," Gyrich sniffs.

"But very astute speculation," Dr. Craig says, getting involved in the discussion for the first time. "We never closed off the receivers that accepted data from the centis. That information was fed directly into the computers. It might be interesting to see what's been coming through that channel."

Dr. Andrews sits down at a terminal, his usual fear momentarily forgotten. His fingers fly across the keyboard, calling up batches of data from the computer. "All the centi data has been scrambled!" he announces. "The computer has classified it as restricted information. It's demanding a password."

"We've got to discover that password!" Dr. Laughlin says grimly.

"What should I try?" Dr. Andrews asks.

"Try 'scum-sucker,' " Jesse hisses, flashing an angry look at Gyrich.

"Try 'ninja,' " Michael pipes up.

"Try 'loonie tunes,' " Wolverine mutters.

If you or your team discovered a secret code name from the Hand or the Sentinel, turn to **84**. If not, turn to **54**.

You can't tell what it is that disturbs you **182S** about the cavern, but you know you had better discover what is going on before you yourself are discovered. So you give Nightcrawler a nod, whispering, "Go ahead—but no grandstanding!"

"I will be a good boy," he promises, then teleports away.

You see him reappear on a ledge above the pit. All seems well, but then you receive a shock. From the pit, a metallic voice booms, "Warning—mutant in vicinity! Identification: Nightcrawler. Capture immediately!"

Nightcrawler disappears from the ledge. You expect him to teleport back to your side, but a moment later, he reappears on the ledge overlooking the pit. He teeters precariously, then collapses, unconscious.

Why couldn't he teleport? you wonder. Then it dawns

171

on you. The maps you studied in the control room, indicated that the mass field went straight down into the ground. You are near the base's foundation, and the mass field is between you and the pit. "Nightcrawler could teleport across it, but he couldn't return, just like when he tried to teleport from the boat to the shore. The attempt was too great a strain."

You look on in horror as a dozen centis hover up to the ledge where Kurt lies helplessly and reach out with tiny steel appendages to grab his clothing, his hair, his tail. Then they float down with their prisoner and carry him through a passage at the opposite end of the cavern.

Nightcrawler might be your only way. Even if he weren't, you can't leave him a prisoner of the centi-bots. Risking detection, you creep along the edge of the room, following Kurt's captors. Fortunately, the light is dimmer near the outer edges of the room, and you manage to reach the other side without being spotted.

You slip into the passage and follow the sound of humming centi-bots. The noise suddenly rises in pitch, and you duck behind a rock as several centis float by. When they've passed, you continue down the tunnel until it ends in a small chamber, full of rotting lumber. Kurt lies at the foot of a pile of two-by-fours, held immobile by a device you are familiar with—inhibitor manacles. Your friend seems to be regaining consciousness, but the metal bindings about his torso, arms, and legs prevent him not only from walking, but from teleporting as well.

Drawing out your lockpicks, you creep toward Nightcrawler and start working on his bindings. In a moment, Kurt's eyes blink open. "Storm!" he gasps. "Thank heaven!"

"Shush, my friend. This shouldn't take long."

Kurt lies there patiently while you try to manipulate the locks on the manacles, but you have no luck. "They must be magnetic locks," you tell him. I shall have to find the key."

"Ororo! Look out!" Nightcrawler shouts.

You roll to one side with lightning speed and leap to your feet. A centi-bot with a hypodermic needle is rushing toward you. Grabbing a beam of wood, you prepare to swat at it.

Make a Fighting FEAT by rolling one die and adding the result to your Fighting ability. If the total is 8 or less, turn to **90**. If it is 9 or more, turn to **97**.

183W After a few minutes, the discoloration of your bruises begins to fade. You flex your muscles and twist your joints a bit, noting that the pain has lessened. Add 1 more to your Health points, then turn to **129**.

184R "It could be dangerous," Wolverine warns you.

You shrug. "I've absorbed worse," you reply, thinking of the man-eating dire wraiths you once faced, the most disgusting creatures in your experience. Anxious to prove your usefulness, you must fight down your own fear of losing control of your mind with the memory of how interesting it can be to know the innermost thoughts of others.

You usually simply press your lips against a person you're absorbing, but the idea of kissing a ninja assassin somehow doesn't appeal to you. Instead, you get a firm grip on your prisoner with your left hand, then use your teeth to pull the glove off your right hand and touch your fingertips to the bare hand of the ninja assassin.

Instantly, horrible images of countless dead bodies flood into your head. Your life is no longer your own. You belong to the master, and death is life.

With a shock, you realize that the ninja's body, robbed of its consciousness, is dissolving at your feet. Fear seizes you that you may have absorbed his mind permanently. Then blackness surrounds you.

You must make a Power Absorption FEAT by rolling one die and adding the result to your Power Absorption ability. If the total is 13 or less, turn to **130**. If it is 14 or more, turn **6**.

Apparently Dr. Andrews sees you out of the **185S** corner of his eye, because he manages to dodge your attack. Then he turns his weapon toward you. Certain that something which could hurt Rogue would probably kill you, you scramble for cover.

You must make an Agility FEAT by rolling one die and adding the result to your Agility ability. If the total is 8 or less turn to **175**. If it's 9 or more, turn to **145**.

"Well, spit it out, kid," Wolverine orders. **186R** "We haven't got all night."

You pause for a moment to think. Even though the mind of the ninja is no longer in control of you, you recall it clearly. You are intensely aware of Wolverine—how alert he seems, how he appears to be standing casually but is actually ready for anything at a moment's notice. He is perhaps the finest fighter you have ever seen. These, you know, are the observations of the ninja inside of you. You wish you could fight Wolverine to learn more about his techniques. With effort, you put aside such thoughts and search the ninja's mind for the information Wolverine requires.

"There are another twenty Hand assassins on the island," you tell your partner. "They're hidin' in a secret underground tunnel. Whoever hired them told them about it and gave them a map of every nook and cranny on this island."

"Do they know who's footin' the bill for this operation?" Wolverine asks.

You shake your head. "There is something unusual about this job, however. Usually, when the Hand are hired to kill an individual, they're given a picture of that person, which bursts into flame once they've studied it. This time the order came in over a computer terminal."

You close your eyes, trying to remember everything the ninja saw on the computer terminal. " Code Name: 'X-cellent Death. Fee: One billion U.S. dollars. Assignment: Kill every human on Obar Island,' " you quote from memory. "Then the screen appeared to burst into flame."

"That's just flamin' wonderful," Wolverine growls. "The Hand going high-tech. As if we didn't have enough problems."

"There's one more thing," you whisper.

"What else?"

"They seem to know that the scientists are havin' trouble keepin' up the mass wall. They believe that whoever's hired them is going to lower it somehow. They're waitin' for it t' crash so they can storm the base."

You can feel the ninja's spirit in your mind slip away

from you, even though it has no physical being to return to.

Wolverine's eyes are narrow slits. You can see he's deep in thought.

"Do we go after their secret base, boss?" you ask.

Your partner shakes his head. "As much as I'd love to tear into twenty ninjas, we can't afford that pleasure just yet. Jesse said her problem with the mass wall had something to do with the computer. Something tells me someone is messin' with it. Storm will have to be warned. You'd better fly us back there right away."

"Ah wonder what Storm and Nightcrawler have been up to while we've been gone . . ." you muse.

Turn to **14**.

187S

As you watch Wolverine destroy one after another of the mini-robots, you find yourself thinking, *These things are more horrible than a swarm of rats!*

You realize just how vulnerable you are without your power to control weather. You are not frightened, however. Five or six of the mechanoids fall at Wolverine's feet, just so many pieces of scrap now.

With fighters like Wolverine, I could probably command this team from an armchair, you muse. But Wolverine wouldn't accept the position of team leader, and he willingly follows your orders. You steel yourself against the rush of robots that make it past the Canadian mutant.

The metal spheres hover overhead for a moment, and then, almost unbelievably, they flee back over the hill, even though the majority of them remained unharmed.

Add 2 to the group's Karma Pool on Wolverine's behalf, for routing the mini-robots. Then turn to **5**.

188W

You crash into the ninja, but you are a second too late. Your foe has already blown the *metsubishi* powder into Rogue's face. You can smell its foul poisonous odor. Rogue begins gagging and gasping for air.

You crouch in a defensive stance ready to keep all the ninja away from Rogue.

"Hang in there, kid," you think, hoping she will survive without attention while you are forced to deal with the enemy. Turn to **125**.

189R Several moments after breathing the powder the ninja blew at you, you are finally able to take another breath that does not send you into coughing fits. Your lungs feel as though they are on fire, and your muscles make little uncontrollable twitches. Wolverine is fighting the two ninja alone, and you don't want to be left out of the battle.

The moment one of the ninjas gets his weapon caught between Wolverine's claws, you lunge toward him, hoping to grab him in a bear hug.

You must make an Agility FEAT by rolling one die and adding the result to your Agility ability. If the total is 8 or less, turn to **107**. If it is 9 or greater, turn to **62**.

190W You swing one broad fist at the ninja in front of you, but the assassin ducks under your blow effortlessly. The second ninja draws his sword and prepares to strike, but with a *snikt*, you unsheathe the claws of your right hand and block the sword. At the same instant, you launch a roundhouse kick at the first ninja, wondering, *Is Nightcrawler going to get in on any of this action, or is he just going to sit in that tree all night?*

Turn to **21**.

191W You slash straight through the Sentinel's wrist, and its fingers spring open. Nightcrawler teleports to your side to help, but Michael seems uninjured. As a matter of fact, he rolls out of the metal hand with his sonic pistol held ready. "Thanks!" he says, his eyes bright with excitement, oblivious to the danger all about him. He fires at another swarm of centis, and several blow up overhead, showering you with centi parts.

"I will keep an eye on Captain Danger, here," Nightcrawler offers pulling the boy away by the shoulders. "Finish your job, *mein Freund*."

"Thanks," you say to Kurt. Waving your claws in Michael's face, you order, "Stay back!" Then you turn to polish off the Sentinel. Turn to **142**.

192R
Wolvie's always tellin' me t' be more careful, you think as your fingers brush against the tree leaves. *Ah shoulda listened to him,* you chastise yourself, unable to get a grip about the branch to halt your descent.

Turn to **146**.

193R
Your boot catches awkwardly on a tree stump and sends you sprawling to the ground next to Wolverine and Storm. You feel several barbs thump into you, but they bounce right off your invulnerable body.

Wolverine and Storm do not fare quite so well, though. Several shurikens have found their target and bury themselves in their skin or tear through their costumes. Subtract 6 from Wolverine's Health points and 3 from Storm's.

"Are you okay?" you ask your companions.

"I've had better days," Wolverine mutters. Turn to **57**.

194S
For months now, you have watched Da Costa and Wolverine rubbing each other the wrong way, and the reason is obvious: They are too much alike. Both are aggressive and both need to be the best. Still, you can tell that beneath Roberto's arrogance, he admires the X-Men's best fighter, though he would die before admitting it to Wolverine.

"Bobby, listen to me very carefully," you begin. "I

want you to put yourself in Wolverine's place. As team captain, his job is to lead his team to victory. His goal is honorable, therefore he must reach it. Your goal is to hit the ball. You should concentrate only on your goal, not on his. Don't think about Wolverine; don't think about what *he* does to reach *his* goal. Think only of what *you* must do. If you keep your head clear, you will reach your goal."

The young Brazilian looks up at you in surprise. You've struck a chord in him, you can tell. "Yes, ma'am," he says, nodding respectfully.

Behind De Costa's head, you see Magneto raise his eyebrows at you in approbation. With a smile, you turn and walk back to your base.

Wolverine does indeed try to psych Roberto out by pitching inside, but the young man miraculously keeps his cool as the ball speeds close by his body. Finally, Wolverine is forced to pitch his fastball to avoid walking the batter.

Roberto hits a line-drive single. You breathe a sigh of relief, more pleased with Roberto's victory over his own temper than with your increased chance of winning the game.

Peter Rasputin, alias Colossus of the X-Men, comes up to bat, and there is nothing Wolverine can do to keep the sturdy Russian mutant from bringing your team's victory. Peter hits a homer way out into the brush behind the outfield. While Nightcrawler hacks through the tall grass searching for the ball, you, Rogue, Roberto, and Peter all run to home plate at your leisure, accepting slaps on the back from the fifth member of your team, Sam Guthrie of the New Mutants.

Wolverine comes up to congratulate you on your win.

" 'Roro, just what did you say to that kid, anyway?" he mutters, indicating Roberto with a toss of his head.

You shrug, trying to appear modest. "Just a little woman-to-man talk." You walk off, the cheers of your teammates ringing in your ears as Nightcrawler returns to Wolverine's side, carrying the baseball. Turn to **150**.

A sudden insight comes to you. While you **195W**
were gone, Rogue might have tried to absorb the prisoner's consciousness to discover his secrets, but instead fell prey to his will.

It all fits. She looks and smells like Rogue, but she sure don't talk or stand the way Rogue does, you think. *I've got only one chance to help her get control of herself again.*

Tensing your muscles, you leap toward Rogue before your teammate can attack.

Turn to **44**.

"No," you reply. "I do not think we should be **196S**
taking any unnecessary risks this evening. We will stay together."

Although Wolverine appears annoyed, you see Rogue nod her approval. *She may make a good leader herself one day,* you think. Turn to **11**.

To your vast relief, Nightcrawler decides to **197S**
stay with you rather than go after the Sentinel alone. "Ah, well, the better part of valor and all that." He crouches on the ground to wait with you for Wolverine and Rogue, twitching his tail restlessly, like a cat.

You don't have to wait long. From above, a voice suddenly asks, "Y'all waitin' for the bus?"

Rogue lands beside you with Wolverine in her arms. She sets her passenger down gently.

"What're you doin' out here, sweetheart?" Wolverine asks.

Briefly you relate your discovery of the secret cave and the Sentinel. "We have been waiting for you before we took care of it."

"Mighty neighborly of you," Rogue jokes.

"What have you been up to?" you ask Wolverine.

"We tussled with some ninjas—the Hand, to be specific. There are more of them out there, but we haven't found them yet. Thought we should report to you first."

"I'm glad you did," you reply. "We need to take care

of that Sentinel, and Kurt has been chomping at the bit."

"I'm the excitable type," the blue-furred X-Man says with a grin.

"Nightcrawler, teleport Rogue and me in first, then come back here for Wolverine."

"Here," Wolverine says handing you Jesse's subsonic pistol. "You might need this."

Nightcrawler teleports you and Rogue into the cavern and returns with Wolverine moments later.

"Where is he?" Rogue whispers.

"Lying in that pit, having his nails buffed by the centis," Nightcrawler answers.

"A sittin' duck, eh?" Wolverine grins.

"Can we go get him now?" Nightcrawler asks.

"Have fun, children," you say.

Nightcrawler teleports away. Rogue lets loose a rebel yell and flies off.

"I hope there's somethin' left when I get there," Wolverine growls, then charges toward the pit.

You hear a loud crashing sound, which you realize must be Rogue, slamming her invulnerable body into the robot. Nightcrawler teleports back above the pit, with his body wrapped around the head of the Sentinel. He has teleported pieces of mechanical objects away from their main body before, but never anything this large. A shower of sparks shoots up from the pit, while wires shoot out crazily from the Sentinel's neck, sizzling loudly.

Kurt has succeeded in decapitating the monster, but it seems to have done him in. He lies across the top of the Sentinel's head, while swarms of centis charge toward him, intent on avenging their destroyed leader. You fire at them with the subsonic pistol. Several blow up immediately, others fall to the floor, while still others scatter to the darker recesses of the cavern.

"Glad to see you decided to join us," Nightcrawler says, looking up from the Sentinel's head.

"Are you all right?" you ask.

"Just resting," he says. "I think I overdid it a little.

You look so serious when you aim that thing," he teases, pointing at the pistol.

"Even when I had my super powers, I took no pleasure in smashing things the way the three of you seem to."

"We'll have to get you in a more adventurous mood."

Brandishing the subsonic pistol, you move toward the edge of the pit. Wolverine has turned what's left of the Sentinel into a mass of spaghetti wires and slivered metal, while Rogue continues to grab and squish any centis that venture near him.

"I think it's time to be get back to the base now," you call out.

"Awww!" Rogue complains.

"Better do as the boss lady says," Wolverine urges. Nightcrawler teleports Rogue and you back aboveground, near the entrance of the scientists' base, then disappears again. A moment later, he returns with Wolverine.

"There is still a lot of work to do," you tell the others. "Providing, of course, that Jesse can get Gyrich to let us back through the mass wall."

"Gyrich is here?" Wolverine snarls.

You nod wordlessly, hoping that your calm will set an example for the others, especially the hot-tempered Wolverine. Turn to **17**.

Just as you try to land a good, solid blow to **198R** the two Hand assassins before you, a blur of movement knocks one of your targets aside.

You cry out with surprise, but recover quickly. The other ninja is also startled, which gives you an opportunity to grab him. With your hand firmly around his wrist, you pull the sword from his grasp.

Wolverine turns and picks up a small box dropped by the ninja he just subdued.

"Watch out for these little gems, kid," he tells you as he sniffs the box.

Your prisoner struggles futilely to pull himself free

from your grasp. "What is it?" you ask.

"It's called a *metsubishi*, and it's filled with poison. If you breathe it in, say your prayers for the last time."

"Wolverine! Look out!" you gasp as a fifth Hand charges from the bushes with his sword aimed at your partner.

Wolverine hardly needs your warning, however. He spins, slamming his foot out and up, directly into the ninja's chin, before you even finish speaking. The ninja slumps to the ground with his sword beneath him.

"Thanks," Wolverine says, "but I heard him coming."

"What do I do with this one?" you ask, shaking your prisoner.

"Hang on to him for a moment," Wolverine orders. Turn to **79**.

199R

You nearly shout with relief when Storm says, "Rogue, you go along with Wolverine. Nightcrawler will stay here with me."

The stuffy underground chamber and long explanations were beginning to put you to sleep. You long for some action in the cool night air, and action is always what you find when you go anywhere with Wolverine.

After giving Wolverine the subsonic pistol, Storm watches the two of you follow Jesse out of the room.

The path through the corridors is just as confusing as it was when you came in. Finally, you reach the door leading outside, but when Jesse enters the code on the control panel, the door only swooshes halfway open, then whines as though it's jammed by something.

"What the heck?" Jesse mutters as she slips out the partially opened door.

You and Wolverine follow her quickly. Embedded in the door, keeping it from opening any farther, is a sharp-edged, flat piece of steel shaped into an eight-pointed star.

"A shuriken!" you whisper, recognizing the deadly weapon instantly. Using the blade of a Swiss Army

knife, Jesse pries the star out of the door. The portal opens all the way as the piece of steel clinks to the ground.

"Don't touch it!" Wolverine warns as you bend down to retrieve the item. Jesse hands you a small pair of tweezers, which you use to pick up the star. Gingerly, Wolverine takes hold of the shuriken at its center and sniffs it. "You don't want to cut yourself with this," he says. "It's poisoned!"

"Have we stepped into a bad martial arts flick or what?" Jesse asks.

"You better keep that mass field up," is all Wolverine says as he wraps the metal star in a handkerchief, then holds up the wrapped weapon. "This could only have gotten in the door between the time you closed it and the moment the shield went back up. Whoever's out there will be faster next time. Come on, kid," Wolverine says to you as he tucks the shuriken into his belt and walks away from the safety of the shielded building.

"Good luck!" Jesse whispers from the doorway.

"You, too, shugah," you whisper back as you hurry forward to catch up to Wolverine, already on the prowl.

Overhead, the moon is nearly full, but the sky has turned cloudy, so there are moments when you can see all around you quite clearly and other times when you are lost in the darkness.

With the subsonic pistol at the ready, Wolverine stands on the slope of the hillside where you fought the troop of centi-bots. He breathes in the air slowly, analyzing all the scents.

All you can smell is wood smoke mixed with a few lingering fumes of smoldering rubber and gasoline.

Wolverine turns to you, looking very grim. "We're dealin' with the Hand," he says.

"What makes you so sure?" you ask.

"The way the guard was stabbed—the poison on the shuriken," your partner replies.

"My, oh, my! That should make for an interestin' evenin'!" You have fought ninja assassins before, but the Hand are reputed to be the best in the world.

"Don't get cocky, girl," Wolverine warns. "They've got ways to take care of even you, and if they get past the two of us, Ororo and Kurt are goin' to be hard-pressed to protect those people back there."

Wolverine starts moving silently down the hillside. Keeping up with him is no problem, but you find it hard to move as stealthily as he does.

"You look a li'l nervous, Wolvie," you tease. "What makes these Hand guys so special?"

"They have no souls," Wolverine replies. "They sell them to become members of the guild. Then they're just extensions of the evil. They don't kill for the money, or even for some perverse pleasure. They just kill."

"But their leaders must have some reason!" you argue.

"Some say they're after world domination."

"Well, at least that sounds pretty typical," you joke.

Wolverine does not smile. "Others say they are ruled by the devil."

"Oh," you murmur, and a shiver runs down your spine. Once you would have dismissed a story like that as a myth, but you've seen and battled against other equally mythical beings since you've joined the X-Men.

"Are we headin' anywhere in particular?" you ask.

"I picked up a man's scent as soon as we got away from the base—probably a guard posted to watch the door. I think he's headin' back to join his buddies and report on us. We're following his scent."

You neither hear, see, nor smell anyone around you, but if Wolverine says someone is out there, you know it's a safe bet. After picking your way through the devastated forest for half an hour, you finally reach another area untouched by the fire.

"I don't see anythin' that could act as a firebreak," you whisper. "Could the blaze have just petered out?"

Logan shakes his head. "*They* stopped it . . . somehow."

Suddenly, an agonized scream pierces the air. "That came from the forest!" you gasp. Without hesitation, you fly into the trees in the scream's direction.

Not far off, you spot a small clearing in the moonlight. Tied to a tree at the edge of the clearing is the body of a man. His head rolls forward and hangs loosely, as though he's just passed out.

You veer instantly in your flight toward the tree, but just as you are about to touch down to the earth, you spot a glint of metal on the ground. *Some sort of booby trap!* you realize immediately. *Won't hurt me, but could kill the prisoner.* Unable to stop your descent in time, you grab for a tree branch to try to keep from setting off the trap.

Make an Agility FEAT by rolling one die and adding the result to your Agility ability. If the total is 7 or less, turn to **192**. If it is 8 or more, turn to **22**.

200N With lightning reflexes, you turn in midair so that the beam of Storm's flashlight illuminates the ground below you. The moment you see it, you teleport down to a few inches above the bottom. "Infinitely preferable to falling thirty feet," you declare as you shine your light up the shaft.

"Agreed!" Storm replies.

Despite your jaunty air, you are still shaking from the close call. Turn to **51**.

201W As you walk away from the Sentinel toward the others, you hear Michael explaining to Storm how the remaining centis could be used to attack the Hand. "We programmed them to attack anyone who wasn't wearing a special identification tag. The Sentinel must have overridden that command to make them attack us anyway. Without the tag, the centis can't tell one person from another."

"That must be why we found a sonic pistol on one of the Hand ninjas," Nightcrawler says to you. "The ninja were hired by the Sentinel, but the centis didn't understand that."

"The Sentinel didn't really care if the Hand assassins died tryin' to carry out Project X-cellent Death," Rogue adds. "But how did the Sentinel get here, and how did it get in touch with the Hand?"

"It could be a Sentinel we've fought before—perhaps one from our battles with the Hell Fire Club," Nightcrawler suggests.

"That sounds likely," Storm agrees. "It must have been unable to return to its original base, and so it tunneled into this cave to hide. Its master probably considered it beyond repair and sealed it inside. Unfortunately, the research lab was later built over the same site. The centis must have come in through another cave entrance."

"Yeah," Michael says, nodding. "When the Sentinel heard the centis, it summoned them here and commanded them to repair it."

"The centis talk?" Rogue asks.

"Well, on different frequencies. They tell the computer what they're doing, and the computer tells us—that is, when it's working right. The computer has been doing some weird things lately, like messing up Jesse's energy program. The computer can make phone calls to transfer data automatically. The Sentinel got the centis to tell the computer to call the Hand."

"I think we may be in the realm of speculation now," Nightcrawler says.

"No," Michael insists, shaking his head. "When the Sentinel ordered the centis to tell the Hand to continue Project X-cellent Death, the centis all talked to the computer. Didn't you here that funny clattering noise they made?"

"I guess you have a better ear for it than us, kid," you

break in, studying Michael carefully, just as you did when you first met him.

Storm begins chiding the boy for risking his life by following you down into the tunnels. "I locked that door above for a reason. How did you get past it?"

"I just crawled under it. I helped here, though, didn't I?"

"You might have been killed—"

You interrupt Storm's lecture. "C'mere, Mikey," you order.

"Don't call me Mikey," the boy says.

"All right. C'mere, Michael," you say with a grin.

Warily, the boy approaches you. You take his sonic pistol away from him and hand him your own. "See that centi near the ceiling? Hit it for me."

Michael shrugs. "Sure!" As Michael fires the pistol, the weapon's grating noise sounds about you, and the centi drops to the cave floor.

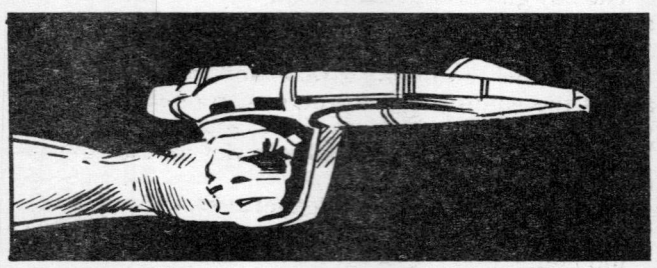

"Now the one over by that red rock," you suggest. Michael drops the second target as easily as the first.

"You think his marksmanship means something, Wolverine?" Storm asks.

"You mean like I'm a mutant?" Michael asks excitedly.

"It is a remote possibility," Storm says. "But more likely, it is a skill you've learned by practice. That, too, is something to be proud of."

"I watched him shooting, Storm," you say. "Nothing

personal, Michael, but your aim is lousy. Besides," you add, holding out two batteries for everyone to see, "the gun ain't loaded."

Michael checks the pistol to reveal the empty battery chamber. "Hey!" he exclaims, surprised. "How could it fire without—"

"Whoa! This is goin' too fast for me!" Rogue says.

"Michael," Storm says, taking the pistol from his hands, "try to hit the centi over by the passageway."

"How?" Michael demands.

"Use your mind," you tell him.

Michael stares at the centi until his eyes bug, but nothing happens.

"Pretend you're holding the gun. Point your finger," you suggest.

Michael follows your suggestion, but he can't help giggling. "I feel silly."

"You look a little silly, too," you tell him.

The boy glares at you. Suddenly, a low rumbling fills the air and a rock wall behind your shoulder begins to crumble.

"From the condition of that wall, I'd say he can adjust the volume and do more than one frequency," you guess. "Probably hears all the sound waves, too."

"A sonic transmitter!" Nightcrawler exclaims, grinning.

"You mean I did that?" Michael asks, looking awed. "I'm a mutant?"

You nod.

"Wow!" Michael exclaims.

"We're going to have to keep an eye on him," Storm says.

"And make sure Gyrich doesn't find out," Rogue adds.

"First, I suggest we get out of this dump," you say.

"Good idea!" Nightcrawler agrees. He teleports Storm and Rogue to the surface first.

While you wait for Kurt to return, you tell Michael, "I've got a piece of advice for you, kid. Follow it, and you may grow up to be an X-Man, too."

"Yes, sir?"

"The advice is, the game isn't over till it's over."

"Huh?" Michael looks blank.

"The game is over," you tell him.

"And we won—right?" he asks.

"Right!" you agree. Your adventure is over.

202S Keeping very still, you try to fight off your annoyance at being so helpless. "These ninjas will make it very difficult to use the centi-scan," you whisper.

"I can backtrack around them and attack them," Wolverine suggests.

Turn to **196**.